DEBORAH MACKIN

Getting back in shape

photography by
Ruth Jenkinson

A Dorling Kindersley Book

LONDON, NEW YORK, MUNICH,
MELBOURNE, DELHI

Senior editor: Liz Coghill
Art editor: Nicola Rodway
Project editor: Susannah Steel
Project art editor: Nick Harris
DTP designer: Karen Constanti
Production controller: Heather Hughes
Managing editor: Anna Davidson
Managing art editor: Emma Forge
Photography art direction: Sally Smallwood
Jacket designer: Nicola Powling
Jacket editor: Jane Oliver-Jedrzejak

Always consult your doctor before starting any fitness and
nutrition programme if you have any health concerns.

First published in Great Britain in 2003
By Dorling Kindersley Limited
80 Strand, London, WC2R 0RL
A Penguin Company

012002020

A CIP catalogue record for this book is available
from the British Library.

ISBN 0 7513 7360 5

Reproduced by Colourscan, Singapore
Printed and bound by Star Standard, Singapore

See our complete catalogue at
www.dk.com

contents

author's introduction

I have been teaching dance and fitness classes for nearly 20 years, and whilst I have enjoyed instructing firemen, football and rugby players and scores of other male students, women – and particularly mothers – are my inspiration for this book. My aim is to help you become and remain fit and well, and to begin your rehabilitation, restoration, and inspiration after having children.

Twenty years ago, unprecedented interest in teaching keep fit in a new way led to a massive growth in all sorts of physically challenging classes. The availability of dance, fitness, yoga, self-defence classes and a multitude of other options has allowed many women to have fun exercising in a positive and satisfying way. For anyone who hated school sports, it is a relief and a joy to exercise without being expected to be the fastest or best. Encouraging people to enjoy their bodies and find release from the daily stresses of work or family is the most satisfying aspect of my teaching.

Hundreds of women tell me that doing their preferred exercise class is essential to their wellbeing, that it gives them a sense of balance and physical enjoyment. For many, it helps keep them sane. These are the converted – they know that being fit is worth the effort. Being a mother doesn't mean that you have to forgo this experience, nor does it mean it is too late to start – now is the ideal time to begin getting fit, whatever your circumstances.

Within these pages I have included both effective and essential exercise direction and information on weight control, fat loss, food fads, and nutritional facts to help you achieve and maintain long-term energy and vitality. From coping with a Caesarean birth to avoiding osteoporosis, this book will enable you to take responsibility for your future wellbeing. I have tried to pare down information to the most effective exercises and vital advice since being a mother does not leave time for unnecessary activities!

Remember – do not think that exercise and nutrition are luxuries that you don't have time for. They are a priority. Set time aside: 10 minutes, three times a week, is a good start. Make a plan and try to protect the time you set aside from the rest of the day's pressures. Getting started is the hardest part, but be reassured that if you do lose your way you can get started again and again.

So if you need motivation, instruction, and advice on getting back into fitness and good health after having children, this book is for you. Whether your baby is 10 days or 10 years old, I hope you will be encouraged to get moving.

Enjoy,

Deborah

getting started

A good exercise programme should be safe, effective and enjoyable, and you should aim for quality of movement over quantity. The exercises that I've included in this book are popular because they work: perform these exercises and you will notice some improvements instantly, while other benefits will be more long term.

GET READY

- Choose well-fitting, supportive trainers, a good sports bra *(see p.103)* and comfortable clothing in light layers, ideally made of cotton
- Keep your kit in a bag or in one place ready for the moment you are free to exercise. You may also like to include hand or ankle weights in your kit, and a notebook and a watch to record your progress
- Always include a bottle of water in your kit bag
- If you have wooden floors you will need to use a foam mat, non-slip rug or a thick towel or blanket
- Choose upbeat music for rhythm and motivation, and slow, calming music for stretching and relaxing
- Have a clear space to exercise, preferably with a mirror, where you won't be disturbed

motivation and direction

For most us who are mothers, it's often easy to ignore our own requirements entirely when we are unable to focus on ourselves for more than a few minutes without interruption from our children. It is months, sometimes even years, after our children are born before many of us are able to get into a regular fitness routine again.

Getting Back in Shape is realistic and effective, with exercises and advice that can be of use for the rest of your life. If you have only five minutes free, there are simple exercises in this book for you to do that will train your

Keep your kit together in one place

muscles, enable you to perform more efficiently and help you to feel more satisfied with your body. Keep the book out, dip into it whenever you can and think of it more as a life tool, not a postnatal baby book.

book structure

Getting Back in Shape has three parts. Part One deals with the first weeks after childbirth and concentrates on those parts of the body made vulnerable by pregnancy and childbirth. There are three areas of the body that can be greatly helped by doing specific exercises: the pelvic floor, the back and the abdominals. The muscles of the pelvic floor and the abdominal muscles have been stretched and weakened during pregnancy and birth, and exercising correctly will help speed recovery. Mobility exercises and stretching will help relieve aches and release tension in the back – a frequent problem after labour and during the early weeks of breastfeeding your baby.

Part Two is for women who have learnt the basics in Part One, and for those mothers who have been to see their GP for the six-week check-up following childbirth. It contains five sections that target specific needs. Firstly, energizer exercises warm up the whole body, offering a gentle workout if you are in a hurry, or a thorough warm-up if you are going on to do further exercise or another section of Part Two.

The lower body workout that follows offers selective toning and strengthening exercises that improve the definition of your lower body, as well as training the cardiovascular system. If you require an aerobically challenging workout, add on any of the lower body life activities.

The third section focuses on the upper body and contains light resistance exercises for a strong, beautifully defined upper body and back.

Meanwhile, the challenging abdominals workout should enable you to reverse the effects of child-bearing on your body. Well-trained abdominal muscles will support the back and aid good posture.

A good stretch sequence to finish with should refresh you and help you to relax, relieve any muscle tension and increase your range of movement.

These five sections in Part Two can be performed individually or altogether, and there are also suggestions for extending your workout further to complement your training – activities such as walking, swimming, running and dancing. Pick and mix from this versatile and progressive fitness programme to maximize your time, energy and fitness, but always start with a warm-up, and allow the body to cool down at the end for at least five minutes. If your plans to exercise go awry, remember that you can start over and over again.

With Part Three dedicated to comprehensive advice on good nutrition, you will have all the knowledge you need for complete health and fitness.

WHY USE A MIRROR?

It is very difficult to improve joint alignment and posture if you cannot see exactly what you are doing, so try to exercise in front of a mirror – preferably a full-length one.

Get into the habit of checking not how you look but whether your shoulders are level or not. Are they relaxed or hunched up by your ears? Is your pelvis neutral and are your knees soft? Have the patience to learn good posture this way, and to be precise with all your positions and directional movements. Precision comes from practice, as does moving gracefully and efficiently.

Stretching for five minutes can make a difference

01

THE FIRST
SIX WEEKS

Part One deals with the first weeks after childbirth and helps you strengthen those parts of your body that have been made most vulnerable by pregnancy and childbirth. The areas in need of attention are the pelvic floor, the abdominal muscles, and your posture. Start these simple but effective mobility exercises and stretches shortly after the delivery to speed your recovery, improve your circulation and give relief from backache.

advice and guidance

Your body has recently been through huge changes, and it will take several months for you to regain your pre-pregnancy weight, tone, shape and hormonal levels. Your joints and back are still soft and vulnerable so exercise is required to rebuild your strength, but you do need to take care and be patient. Listen to your body more carefully than ever – real harm can be done if you do too much, too soon.

TAKING CARE OF YOUR BACK

- Don't carry anything heavier than your baby for the first six weeks
- Bring your baby to your level when changing or feeding (take your baby to the breast, not the other way round)
- Use cushions to support your back when driving, typing or breastfeeding
- Strengthen the upper back (see pp.68–79) to help support the extra weight of your breasts
- Carry your baby in a sling across your chest rather than on one hip

rest and replenish

Now is not the time to worry about losing weight, but to focus on gentle stretches and mobility exercises, good nutrition and getting as much rest as possible during these first few weeks after your baby's birth. Remember that your joints are still unstable and the muscles of the abdomen and the pelvis are weak and overstretched. Your breasts are heavier and your back may be aching more than usual as you get to grips with feeding your baby.

why these exercises?

Many women find it daunting to even think about exercise at this time but it's important to remember that any exercise is better than none at all. Just five or 10 minutes a day spent on the crucial areas such as posture, the pelvic floor and the back will be so beneficial in the long run.

Three exercises can be performed immediately after the birth: pelvic floor squeeze (see p.17) in any position, pelvic tilt (see p.24) in any position and abdominal compressions (see p.24) in any position. These are most important for the speedy recovery of the pelvic floor and abdominals. Even if you have had a Caesarean section you can do these exercises as soon as you want after you have given birth.

The mobility and stretch exercises in this chapter will improve your circulation and help relieve aches and tension. Do these exercises as soon as you feel ready.

go at your own pace

Everyone has a different level of fitness, a different birth, and different recovery levels, and this initial period after the birth can be exhausting and demanding. Try not to think of the exercises in this section as another chore, and don't stop doing them just because you can't manage them all at once – you won't get back in a day. Getting started is the hardest part of getting your body back; have faith! Some benefits are immediate, but some are subtle and slow to happen.

If you can do this programme every day you will see results quickly, but if that's impossible, once a week is better than nothing. Do a little when you can and capitalize on your good days.

getting onto the floor

The job of the abdominals (abs) is to support the spine, but after childbirth these muscles are stretched and weak, so extra care needs to be taken to protect this vulnerable area when getting up from and down to the floor.

WARNING!

Stop an exercise immediately if you experience any pain or discomfort. Take care to protect the abdominals (abs), the back or an incision as you get up from and down to the floor. Avoid twisting the trunk or bending at the waist, and keep the back straight. Tilt the pelvis forward and tighten the abs before moving, and make your legs work hard.

1 Tighten the abs and step forwards with your right foot. Place both hands on front thigh. Lower left knee to the floor.

2 Lower yourself onto both knees and place your hands on the floor directly under your shoulders.

3 Lower yourself carefully onto one hip while your hands stay in front of you, supporting your weight.

4 Check that the abs are tight as you lower slowly to the floor. To lie on your back, place both feet on the floor, keep knees touching and move body and legs together without twisting. Reverse these actions to get up.

caesarean births

If you have had a Caesarean section, you will be very aware of the discomfort of the incision, not to mention the difficulties of getting in and out of bed, moving around and finding a comfortable position for breastfeeding. However, it will probably encourage you to know that gentle exercise can help speed your recovery.

BREASTFEEDING

Finding a good position for feeding is important. You may have to try several positions to find out what is most comfortable for you, though you will probably have more control sitting on a chair than in bed. Try placing a thick book under one foot and a pillow on your lap to bring your baby up to breast level.

recovery time

During a Caesarean delivery the rectus muscles (*see diagram, p.80*) are drawn apart; after the delivery the muscles are realigned and should recover in the same way as a vaginal delivery. Any numbness and tingling that you may feel around the incision is normal, and the underlying layers of muscle should not be affected. The damage to the abdominal muscles is less severe than many people assume.

Just getting out of bed at least two or three times a day and walking around the house will help your body recover more quickly from the operation. To get out of bed, go slowly and at your own pace. Support your incision with one hand. Roll onto one side, keeping both knees together and with your shoulders, hips and knees all facing one way to avoid twisting. Push up to a sitting position and bring your feet down to the floor. Brace your abdominal muscles with one arm and let your legs do the work to push you upright.

You may well find yourself stooping forward to protect your incision. Try to stand and walk as tall as possible. If it

1 Sit on the floor or bed for ankle exercises. Stretch out one leg and point your toes, then flex your foot. Do this 20–30 times.

2 Then circle the foot 15 times in each direction. Repeat with the other leg.

helps, you can support the incision with one hand as you move around. To get back into bed, get as close as possible to the head of the bed. Brace your abdominals with one arm, sit down on the bed and ease your legs onto the bed, one at a time.

exercising safely

Most of the exercises in Part One are suitable to perform after a Caesarean birth, but go slowly. Always check your posture and alignment, and learn how to get up and down from the floor safely (*see p.*13). If any movement causes you discomfort or pain, then stop immediately. If you can only spare five minutes to exercise each day, then practise neutral pelvis (*see p.*18), pelvic floor squeezes (*see p.*17), abdominal compressions (*see p.*24) and shoulder rolls (*see p.*21).

Other useful exercises to try after a Caesarean section include deep breathing, with the focus on the exhale: support your incision with your hands and instead of coughing, try to "huff". This helps to clear the lungs of any secretions. Gentle ankle exercises (*left*) will increase your circulation and help prevent thrombosis.

WARNING!

Although most of the exercises described in Part One are suitable for women who have had a Caesarean section, one or two exercises are not appropriate. Please read the warnings before you try an exercise.

Walk around the house to help speed your recovery

your pelvic floor

During pregnancy, the pelvic muscles support all the extra weight of the baby, the placenta, and the uterus. After childbirth, these muscles are stretched and weakened. It is therefore very important to exercise the muscles as soon as you possibly can. Even if you have had stitches or a tear, the pelvic floor squeeze will encourage healing. This is the one exercise to perform every day, even on the day of the birth itself.

MAIN AIMS

- Aid recovery from childbirth
- Prevent incontinence and loss of sensation in the pelvic region
- Restore the pelvic floor to its full capability, and re-establish the intensity of a woman's orgasm

the pelvic region

The pelvic floor is a hammock of muscles that supports the bladder, the bowels and the uterus, and assists with the opening and closing of these three organs (*see diagram, right*). Working to restore the full capability of these muscles after childbirth is crucial if you want to avoid incontinence and a loss of sensation in your pelvic region. The pelvic floor is made up of 70 per cent slow-twitch fibres and 30 per cent fast-twitch fibres. Slow-twitch fibres provide stamina and give support to the pelvic area over long periods, while fast-twitch muscles provide strength and speed and improve the reflex action of the sphincter muscles around the vagina and anus. Both slow and fast contractions must be practised to fully rehabilitate the pelvic floor (*see pelvic floor squeeze, opposite*). Persevere with this exercise, even if it is the only one you can manage at the moment. It will bring real and lasting benefits. Within two or three months you can restore your muscles to their former state.

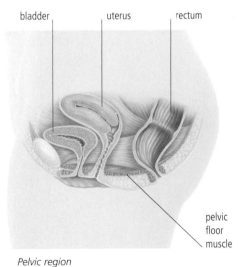

bladder   uterus   rectum

pelvic floor muscle

Pelvic region

SEX AFTER CHILDBIRTH

Many women experience a loss of libido after childbirth. While this is no surprise, it can be difficult for their partners who may be eager to get back to normal. The important thing for you to do is to explain how you feel and to reassure your partner that this is temporary but common. Be aware of how he feels and give him your attention; men's needs are often ignored when a baby is born, so be understanding of each other's feelings. If you have any concerns, talk to your GP.

pelvic floor squeeze

You can perform the pelvic floor squeeze anywhere, although it will be easier to begin on the floor. Aim to perform this exercise several times a day.

1 Lie on your back, feet flat on the floor, knees bent, and pelvis in neutral spine position *(see p.24)*. Relax your face, shoulders and buttocks. Breathe normally.

2 Draw up your muscles in the vagina as if to stop the flow of urine. Squeeze slowly for a count of 10. Repeat 10 times. Contract the muscles as hard as you can. Now squeeze the pelvic muscles fast: squeeze for 1 second and repeat 20 times. Avoid tensing any other areas of the body.

practise the pelvic floor squeeze every day for the rest of your life

posture

Posture is all about the way you hold your body. An ideal posture is one where the skeleton is subjected to the least possible strain. Correct posture protects the body against injury, whereas poor posture can result in stress and strain to ligaments, joints, muscles and bones.

NEUTRAL POSITION

This is the term used to describe the natural curvature of the spine. We have three curves in our spine: cervical, in the neck; thoracic, in the chest area; and lumbar, in the lower back. These curves act as shock absorbers for the spine and give the back its strength. Standing correctly in neutral pelvis position (*see right*) will support the curves of the spine most effectively.

strengthening the abdominals and the upper back will make good posture easy to maintain

neutral pelvis

Maintaining good posture in neutral position requires equal stamina in the abs and back muscles. Check your posture frequently in a mirror.

1 Stand with your feet slightly wider than hip-width apart. Keep your knees soft and find a neutral position for your pelvis so that you are neither arched nor pushed too far forwards. The tail bone should run towards the floor.

2 Imagine pulling your belly button towards the spine and sticking it there with a staple. After a few seconds you will feel the muscles tiring: you are correctly training the abdominal muscles. Now lift your chest, take your shoulders down and back, and lengthen your neck. Imagine that a string is attached to the top of your head and is pulling you up towards the ceiling. Think tall and walk tall.

INCORRECT POSTURE

good posture instantly and dramatically improves your appearance

plié with arm swing

This movement is a rhythmic waking and warming action that opens up the chest, stretches the shoulders and gives you energy. Put on some lively music and work with the rhythm. Breathe deeply. Keep the movement flowing – it has its own momentum. Repeat this movement 10–20 times.

1 Stand with good posture, knees soft, feet hip-width apart and arms crossed.

2 Bend knees. Drop arms down and out. Keep chest lifted and hips below ribs.

3 Swing the arms out to the side and cross them above your head as you stretch your legs and squeeze your buttocks. Look up at your hands.

4 Reverse the action: drop the arms down and outwards as you bend, then stretch the legs. Finish with the arms swinging across the chest.

GETTING STARTED

Muscles stretch best when warm and relaxed. To begin with, you may find yourself holding your breath when you stretch, and even tensing in some areas because you are concentrating. Relax and breathe slowly and deeply. With practice you will find that the optimum time to stretch is when you exhale, for this is when the muscles soften.

neck stretch

After labour, disturbed nights, and tension from sitting in certain feeding positions, these neck stretches bring some relief. You will feel the benefits instantly. They can be done anywhere and anytime throughout the day, even while breastfeeding, but if you can do them in front of a mirror, even better.

1 Stand or sit with your shoulders level and relaxed. Turn your head to the right and look over your shoulder as far as is comfortable.

2 Return your head to start position then turn it to the left. Repeat several times, inhaling through the nose and out through the mouth.

back of neck stretch

Drop your chin to your chest, pull the shoulder blades down and push the chin further down as you exhale. Feel the stretch in the back of the neck and hold the stretch for 10 seconds.

shoulder roll

If you have backache, stand tall to stretch the spine, breathe deeply to restore your energy, and practise this shoulder roll. It is made up of four stretches that mobilize the shoulder joints and help to release tension around the neck. Practise it regularly, and especially after breastfeeding.

1 Sit or stand with good posture, arms relaxed by your sides. Push both shoulders forward.

2 Keeping everything else still, lift your shoulders up towards your ears.

3 Pull the shoulders back, bringing the shoulder blades towards the centre.

4 Bring the shoulders down. The shoulder blades slide down and in, and lift the chest.

stretching relieves muscle tension and increases your range of movement

relieving pain and tension in the back

Ligaments in the back become soft and vulnerable during pregnancy, and breastfeeding or holding your baby for long periods can exacerbate backache. Mobilizing the spine and back muscles will release tension and increase the supply of oxygenated blood, which will hasten your recovery.

TIPS FOR RELIEF FROM BACK PAIN

- Whenever you bend to pick your baby up, practise neutral pelvis position (see p.18), soften your knees and draw in your abdominal muscles
- Keep your back and neck long, lift your head up, and keep your shoulders down
- When you stand up, push up using your thighs
- Never bend at the waist since this puts great strain on the spine

upper back stretch

This stretch is a favourite of mine. Stand with good posture, knees soft, and tilt your pelvis forwards. Interlock your fingers, or hold onto one wrist, and push your hands as far away from your chest as possible. Look down and allow your upper back to relax.

side stretch

Stand with feet slightly wider than hip-width apart, knees soft. Reach the right arm up and lift the torso out of the hips. Bend to the side and exhale. Keep abs tight. Hold, then repeat on other side.

lower back stretch

This stretches the full length of the spine, but you will feel the relief particularly in the lower back. Stand with feet hip-width apart, knees slightly bent, hands on thighs. Contract the abs, drop the chin to chest and curl the pelvis forwards, making the spine as curved as you can. Hold this position for a few seconds and breathe deeply. Relax, straighten, lengthen and repeat whenever you feel low back pain or tension.

hip roll

This exercise mobilizes the lower back and pelvis, releases tautness, relieves lower backache and stimulates more fluid in the joints, making movement easier. With your hands on your waist, draw a big circle with your hips, taking them out to one side and round to the other. Breathe deeply as you repeat the hip roll several times.

abdominals

Your stomach muscles may well be worrying you – they will have stretched by up to 60 centimetres (23 inches)! However, they respond to training and change shape fast. These exercises are progressively more difficult. If you are in any doubt, only do the first two exercises until you have had your six-week check.

FLOOR POSTURE CHECK

Lie on your back with your knees bent and feet flat on the floor. Roll your pelvis forwards and backwards until you find a position in which your back makes light contact with the floor. This is neutral spine position.

abdominal compressions

This is the most important abdominal exercise to do since it shortens and strengthens the transversus muscles (*see p*.80), which stabilizes the spine and flattens the abs. Pull your stomach in as if trying to attach your navel to your spine. Hold this position for five seconds while you breathe normally. Repeat 10 times. Increase the time you hold the compression to 10 seconds.

pelvic tilts

This action also involves the muscles that aid good posture. A pelvic tilt (*right*) will keep stress away from the spine by activating the abdominals. Lie on your back, or stand with good posture. Curl the pelvis forwards so that your tail bone straightens in line with the spine. You will feel the transversus muscles tighten as you tilt the pelvis. Compress the abs to make the muscles work harder and flatter. Hold this position for 5–10 seconds and breathe normally. Relax and repeat whenever you have backache or if you need to lift a heavy object.

retraining your abs

During pregnancy the main abdominal muscles, the rectus abdominus (*see p.*80), may separate. After the birth you may feel a space of 2–4 finger widths between the muscles. This gap closes as the muscles grow stronger. Abdominal compressions and pelvic tilts (*far left*) help speed this process. To see how these muscles are realigning, do a rec check (*left*). If you have a gap larger than two finger widths (including after the six-week check) do not do any twists until it closes.

basic crunch

This strengthens and realigns the rectus abdominus. Work slowly; better four slow and controlled than 10 fast! Keep an eye on your abdominals: if they start to dome, lower the lift slightly to maintain the flatness of the muscles.

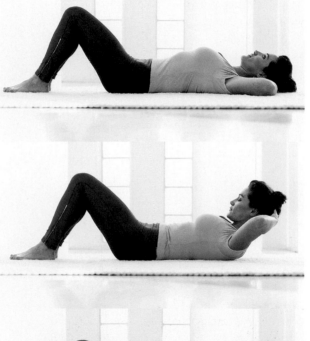

1 Lie in neutral spine position, knees bent, your hands supporting the weight of your head without pulling on your neck. Inhale.

2 Compress the abs down, exhale, and raise your head and shoulders off the floor, keeping the neck long. Release and inhale. Repeat 2–10 times until your muscles ache.

3 This exercise works the oblique muscles that pull in your waist. Exhale and then reach your left hand towards the left ankle. Release, inhale, and lower slowly back to the start position. Repeat 2–10 times on each side until your muscles ache.

relax and stretch

Muscles need stretching to help the body rebalance after pregnancy.
These stretches will help reduce muscle tension and aid relaxation.
Muscle imbalance caused by incorrect alignment during pregnancy
can be easily remedied and prevent poor posture becoming a life habit.

TOP TIPS FOR STRETCHING

- Your movements should be smooth and controlled. Never "bounce" a stretch
- Never stretch cold muscles. Wear comfortable clothing and only stretch when you are feeling warm
- The sensation of a stretch should not be painful; stop if in doubt
- As you hold a stretch you will notice that any discomfort subsides when you relax. Breathe deeply and feel the muscle soften on the exhale
- If you have hard floors, use a foam mat or a thick towel to work on

hamstring and calf stretch

Shortened or tight hamstrings are often responsible for poor posture, restricted movement and back problems. Regular stretching can help improve all of these conditions, and also increase your performance in sport, dance and everyday activities. Feel this stretch in the bulky part of your thigh.

1 Lie with the left leg bent and the left foot on the floor. Hold the back of the right thigh and point the toes.

2 Flex and point the toes of the right foot. Keep your back and hips in contact with the floor at all times.

3 Stretch the leg up, keeping the knee soft. Breathe out as you feel the stretch. Hold for 10 seconds. Lower slowly and repeat with the other leg.

HOLDING A STRETCH

The hormone relaxin, which softens the pelvis in preparation for childbirth, is present in the body during pregnancy and for some months afterwards. This means that during this time the joints are susceptible to overstretching. Normally muscles respond better to longer periods of stretching, but during these first few weeks only a short duration of stretching – between five and 10 seconds – is needed.

quad and hip flexor stretch

Do this stretch standing up or lying on the floor. Given that your breasts will be sensitive, lie on your side rather than your front, with one arm on the floor to support you. Keep the knees in line and your hips stacked one over the other.

1 Bring your left foot towards your buttocks and grasp it with your left hand. Exhale and curl the hips and pelvis forwards to feel the stretch in the thigh and the front of the hip.

2 Hold for 5 seconds. Keep your knees together to ensure a good stretch. Relax and repeat on the other side.

WARNING!

C-section mums should avoid any twisting movement until the incision has healed. If in doubt, leave it out.

body stretch

Initially this exercise stretches the hips, buttocks, and outer thigh. As you lie down, the stretch continues into the trunk, spine, shoulders and neck. Ease into both positions slowly, and feel the muscles relax as you exhale.

1 Lie on your right side, leaning on your elbow. Place the left knee on a pillow or the floor in front of you.

2 Lower your body down, stretch arms out and look back to rear arm. Breathe easily. Repeat on the other side.

back, shoulder and neck stretches

Constantly rounded shoulders result in weakened and overstretched upper back muscles, while shortened hamstrings, hip flexors and quads, and weak abdominals lead to poor sitting and standing posture. This imbalance can be dramatically improved by doing these stretches and abdominal exercises for a few minutes every day.

MAIN AIMS

- Increase the range of movement
- Make daily tasks easier to perform
- Increase performance
- Reduce the risk of injury
- Improve posture
- Reduce muscular tension

cat stretch

You will feel this revitalizing stretch along the length of the spine. Imagine that the head and pelvis are going to meet as you round your spine. Pull the area between the shoulder blades up high and hold for 10–15 seconds.

1 On all fours, position hands under shoulders, your back and pelvis in neutral.

2 Tuck your head and pelvis under and contract the abs. Breathe easily.

c-stretch

This is lateral sideways stretch for the spine. Keep the hips above the knees as you walk your hands to the side to make the spine into a "c" shape.

1 Start on all fours, pelvis in neutral position. Breathe easily. Cross one hand over the other as you walk the hands round to one side.

2 Slowly move your hands round until you feel the stretch all down one side of your body. Repeat on the other side.

shoulders and back

Start this stretch on all fours. Drop your hips back and down without letting your buttocks touch your heels. Slide the arms forwards and rest your forehead on the floor. Relax and enjoy.

inner thigh stretch and neck stretch

To stretch your inner thighs, groin and hips, sit on the floor or on a cushion. Hold the ankles and bring the soles of your feet together (*below*). Keep the chest lifted, your back straight and your head suspended by an imaginary string. Inhale. Lean forward from the hips and exhale. Hold the stretch. Breathe normally. Straighten up, then perform this neck stretch to release tension.

1 Sit with good posture, shoulders down. Look round to the right and drop your chin to your shoulder.

2 Slowly move your head so that your chin rests on your chest. Feel the stretch on the back of the neck.

3 Moving slowly, continue the semi-circle to the left side. Repeat several times.

02

AFTER THE SIX-WEEK CHECK

The exercises in Part Two target specific areas of the body, with separate sections for each area. Each section can be performed individually or as part of a series that comprises a full training programme. With suggestions for incorporating activities to complement your training, this series of exercises provides a progressive, versatile fitness plan. Pick and mix exercises to suit your time and energy levels, but always start with the warm-up and allow at least five minutes to stretch and cool down.

warm-up and energizer exercises

A proper warm-up gradually prepares the heart, brain, muscles and joints for activity, and protects the body against possible injury. The heart will start to deliver more oxygenated blood to the muscles so that you can exercise longer, and with ease. Muscles and tendons become more pliable and effective and the natural lubricant in the joints and the spine, synovial fluid, is released, making greater movement possible.

THE IDEAL WARM-UP

- Mobility exercises take each joint through its full range. This stimulates more fluid in the joint, which allows for easier movement and greater shock absorption
- Pulse-raising exercises are big rhythmic movements that make the heart work harder, improving the body's circulation, warming the muscles and increasing the rate of oxygen flowing around the body
- Stretching muscles increases performance and decreases the risk of injury; muscles are pliable and stretch better when warm

why warm up?

This energizer section is exactly that: if you are feeling sluggish or tired, these exercises will wake you up and warm you up to prepare you for further exercise. You can also use this energizer section on its own as a quick, everyday workout if appropriate.

The lower body exercises in this section are fairly demanding and so are effective in quickly shaping and strengthening legs, hips, and buttocks. By increasing the number of repetitions of these leg exercises, or by adding a few minutes of brisk walking, stepping, or skipping, you can adapt and progress this warm-up to suit your own energy and endurance levels.

Once you feel fitter and want to work out for longer, add on another section such as abdominals (*see pp*.80–89). For aerobic training, add on the lower body section (*see pp*.50–65), and try the activities suggested on pages 66–67 to enable you to make progress in your fitness training gradually each week. Keep on adding different sections to avoid becoming bored or plateauing.

Lying hamstring stretch (see p.49)

PHYSICAL PRECAUTIONS

- Exercise is energizing if you feel flat or lethargic, but if you are really exhausted do not exercise: poor coordination due to fatigue can lead to accidents, as can exercising through pain. If you feel pain, stop, recheck the instructions and adapt the exercise so it feels comfortable – or leave it out
- If you are constantly lacking in energy, the best way to combat this is to train aerobically several times a week. Aerobic exercise will give you more energy and stamina in the short, and long, term
- Dizziness, nausea and breathlessness are signs that you should stop exercising immediately
- Overexertion during exercise will leave you exhausted afterwards, and even on the following day. Muscles that still ache after two or three days are also a sign that you have overdone things

focusing your mind

As well as priming the body for aerobic exercise, the warm-up should be a time to focus your energy, to think about what you want to achieve and how you can make it happen.

If you have attended fitness classes before, you have probably performed many well-organized warm-ups. The advantage of being in one of these classes is that your teacher will have carefully incorporated all the necessary components to prime your body for full exercise – perhaps without your even noticing exactly which groups of muscles you are working. So as you progress through this section try to keep your mind on each movement you do so that you learn about which muscles you are working. Visualize exactly which muscles you are using as you progress through each movement and stretch.

You will also quickly discover which of your muscles are weaker, and which exercises you find easier to do than others. Try to resist taking the easy option all the time. Be aware of any imbalance in your muscle strength and flexibility, and spend longer exercising those weaker areas of your body.

During your warm-up your movements must be controlled and should increase in intensity gradually so that your heart rate rises steadily. After five minutes of energizing movement you should be sweating lightly, and although you will be puffing a little your breathing should be steady. Throughout your training you should still be able to talk. This shows that you are working at the right pace.

overload

Exercise forces the muscles to work harder than usual; this is called overload. It causes a series of changes in the muscles, which quickly results in a more efficient fuel and blood supply in the body. This enables the muscles to work harder. After just a few sessions you will notice how much easier these exercises are and that your recovery time is getting shorter. This is when you will begin to feel and see the benefits and enjoy your progress.

Upper body stretch (see pp.34–35)

MAIN AIMS

- A warm-up is essential, both physically and mentally: use this time to focus
- The abdominals are your centre of power, compress them as you prepare. Feel how crucial they are to controlling all the other parts of the body
- Working through the big muscles of the legs and back will warm, loosen and prepare your body for more action

swing and reach

Take time to learn this exercise, starting with a posture check in front of a mirror. Big movements such as this will wake up your spine, back muscles, buttocks, hamstrings, thighs, shoulders and each side of your body. Repeat several times.

1 Stand with good posture, knees soft, feet hip-width apart. Feel your weight on the balls of your feet. Raise both arms and keep shoulders down. Reach up with the right arm and release. Repeat with left arm.

2 Exhale and let your arms fall forwards as you bend the knees and curve your back and your neck. Let the energy flow through the movement.

reach up high out of your hips and
feel the stretch from the fingertips
right down the side of the body

3 As you reach the end of the swing, relax your head, shoulders, elbows and hands, but keep the abdominals tight.

4 Inhale deeply and swing the arms forwards and upwards. Tighten the abdominals as you bring the torso back to the standing start position.

5 Each time you come to standing, try to reach a little closer to the ceiling. Imagine a string attached to the centre of your head, lifting you taller.

LOWER BODY WORK
- Take care to align knees over feet. Do not allow the knees to shoot out in front of the feet on deep bends
- Look in a mirror to improve the precision of a move
- Use arm movements to generate momentum and energy and aid balance

the slower you work, the more intense a movement becomes

side step

Like the plié (*opposite*), the side step focuses on the buttocks and leg muscles. These exercises require good alignment, coordination and precision to be really challenging, so it's hard to overdo them if you are a beginner. As you improve you can adapt them to a level that suits you. Try to keep your body on a low level. Start by doing 10 wide side steps and aim for 20.

1 Keep spine long, knees bent, chest lifted, abdominals tight and prepare your right foot.

2 Step sideways, wide and low, with your right foot. Drop your hips down and back as you swing your arms forwards.

3 Bring the left foot in and pull both arms in towards the hips. Repeat on the other side.

plié

The plié is simple to follow, but it takes effort to perfect such a graceful movement and requires discipline, strength and stamina. Aim to create one controlled, evenly paced movement. Begin by counting four seconds down, four seconds up for 5–10 pliés, then add 10–20 repeats of two seconds down, two seconds up for a more demanding challenge.

1 Position feet slightly wider than hip-width apart and turn the toes out.

2 Inhale, lift arms out to the sides and bend the knees. Keep heels down, knees over toes, ribs in line with hips, hands soft and shoulders relaxed.

3 Stretch your legs and lift the arms up, squeezing the buttocks and quads as you exhale.

4 Inhale, bend deeply again and bring the arms to sides, then stretch the legs, squeeze the buttocks, bring arms down and lift chest. Repeat.

SQUAT TIPS

- Conditioned buttocks help reduce the risk of knee and back injuries
- The thighs should be parallel to the floor while in a squatting position

squat

This is one of my top ten exercises, an amazingly effective and challenging move that takes practice if you are to do it well without falling over! Until you are confident doing squats, begin by holding on to a door handle or a heavy chair – something at waist height that won't move. Before you start this exercise, position your feet hip-width apart, keep your abdominals tight, your chest lifted and your pelvis in neutral position. Begin with 5–10 repetitions each of slow squats (take about eight seconds for each squat) and medium squats (about four seconds each). Work up to 15–20 repetitions over 10 weeks.

ONE-LEGGED SQUAT

To practise a one-legged squat follow directions as for squat, but place the front foot on a low step or book. Use a support such as a stair rail while you learn. Begin with 5–10 repetitions on each leg; work up to 15–20.

1 Inhale and dip hips down and back. The weight is all on the heels, with the hips way behind the heels. As you bend, swing the arms in front for balance and momentum.

2 Exhale as you stand. Squeeze the buttocks tight and push hips forwards without locking your knees. Pull the arms into the hips.

energizing workout

If you want to use this section as a quick workout and not just a warm-up, you can add on a few extra minutes of energetic exercise at this point. Put on some music and march briskly on the spot, or step up and down the bottom step of your stairs for 2–5 minutes, alternating your leading foot. If you have a rebounder, treadmill or rowing machine, you could spend a few minutes working at a moderate level. You should always be able to talk normally even while doing energetic exercise; if you can't, lower the intensity but do not stop abruptly. Walk on the spot and spend five minutes cooling down, gradually decreasing your workload and then stretching out the muscles.

the wave

This exercise links several
different stretches into
a flowing, energizing
sequence. Until you have
mastered the wave, count
through the movements.
The whole exercise is
16 counts, a count being
1–2 seconds. Go slower
if you wish, but not
faster. This movement
comes alive when each
position flows smoothly
into the next, with the
muscles stretching and
releasing energy back
into your body. So focus
your attention and enjoy
the fluidity of your body
as you move through
each position. Repeat
5–10 times.

1 Take arms up and slightly
  behind the ears.

2 Drop the arms down and
  push them out in front of
  you to stretch the upper back.

3 Pull arms back to lift,
  stretch and open the
  chest. Breathe normally.

this beautiful motion stretches the arms, shoulders, chest, neck, back – and brain!

4 Contract the abs and pull your arms forwards to stretch the upper back and shoulders.

5 Drop the hips back, align knees over feet and slide your hands down the thighs.

6 Contract the abs, curl the pelvis forward and tuck your head down.

7 Keep the chin down, curl up through the spine and stretch the legs and arms.

neck stretches

These two exercises are wonderful for helping release tension and increase the range of movement in your neck. Stand or sit comfortably as you perform them and move slowly, keeping the abdominals tight, the chest lifted and the shoulders down and back. Hold each position for about 10 seconds.

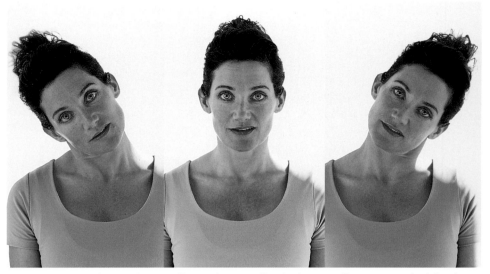

1 Keep your spine long and shoulders down. Tilt head to right side. Feel the stretch on the left side of your neck.

2 Breathe normally. Slowly move your head back to an upright position. Keep your eyes closed if you prefer.

3 Repeat on the left side, tilting your head until you feel the stretch. Keep the rest of your body relaxed. Repeat.

1 Pull your shoulders back and down, lift your chest, and slowly turn to look over your right shoulder. Pause.

2 Bring your head to the centre. Breathe normally throughout the movement.

3 Look round to the left, as far as is comfortable. Pause. Return to the centre and repeat.

shoulder rolls

Stretches such as this are intended to release tensions and relax and revive you, whatever you are doing. Shoulder rolls, like neck stretches, are particularly beneficial to do at the end of the day or even as you sit working.

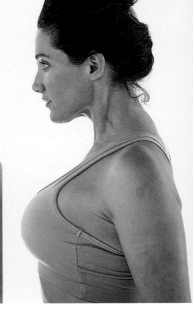

1 Push the shoulders forward to feel the upper back stretch. Hold for 10 seconds. Breathe normally throughout.

2 Lift the shoulders up to the ears and relax the face and neck.

3 Pull the shoulders back. Hold for 10 seconds. Feel the muscles working in the upper back.

4 Slide the shoulder blades down. Keep the chest lifted. Repeat the steps as one smooth sequence of movements.

after driving, or working at a desk or computer, spend five minutes on these exercises to release tension in the head, neck and shoulders

spine side reach

The two directional movements most often neglected are the lateral flexion, or side reach, and rotation, or twist (*opposite*). When mobilizing the spine, don't be tempted to swing with the momentum or to a music beat. You must be able to stop and restart at any point of your stretch. So move slowly in both directions, staying in control as your body moves sideways.

1 Stand tall, feet slightly wider than hip-width apart, knees soft, abs tight. Lift your chest up.

2 Reach out your left arm. Bend to the left as far as you can. Move your body sideways but keep the hips facing forwards. Repeat on other side.

twist

Stand tall with good posture. Compress the abs to keep the hips still. Keep your feet slightly wider than hip-width apart and your knees soft. Do not increase your speed as you become more supple: this twisting movement should be smooth and controlled.

hip roll

Roll your hips when you feel your back aching. This will increase the blood flow and release tension. With your hands on your hips, bend your knees and draw a big circle with your hips. Breathe deeply as you roll several times in each direction.

1 Bend the elbows and lift the arms to chest height. Keep the pelvis neutral. Tighten the abs, lengthen the spine and keep the lower body facing forwards.

2 Slowly turn your head, shoulders and torso as far as you can to one side. Return to centre with slow control. Lift the chest again and repeat 5 times on each side.

stretch the calf muscles regularly and go barefoot when you can

FEET AND ANKLES

The feet and ankles are often neglected in a warm-up. The simple moves on these pages are essential preparation for all sports, including running, dancing, skipping, stepping, and even walking over rough, uneven ground. Such exercises are designed to loosen up and improve the performance of those joints that will be used in a workout, as well as increase the blood supply to muscles to warm them and make them more responsive.

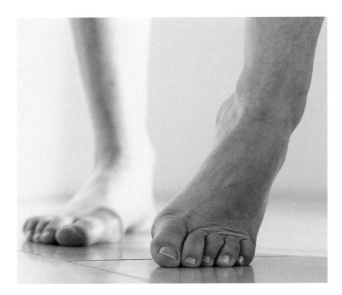

ankle roll

Having suffered from ankle injuries, I always do this movement before any energetic exercise. Stand on one leg with the knees soft and abs tight. With hands on hips, place the ball of the foot lightly on the floor and circle each ankle eight times.

footwork

For this exercise, stand with good posture, feet together, knees soft and abdominals tight.

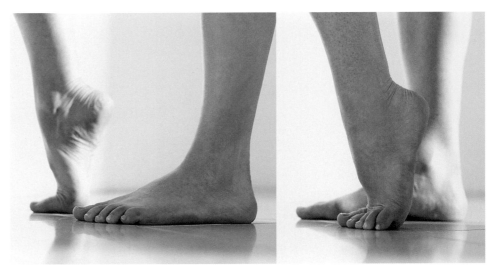

1 Lift up the heel of the right foot and push the arch of the foot forwards, moving your weight onto the ball of the foot.

2 Transfer your weight smoothly from one foot to the other, pushing down onto the floor with the ball of the left foot. Repeat with 10 slow, 10 fast movements.

calf stretches

The calf muscles change their length depending on the activity that you do or do not do. Stretch these muscles before any sport – but only after several minutes of warming exercise. Stand with good posture, feet apart, neutral pelvis. Take a stride back with the right leg, keep the back straight, lean forwards from the hips and put your hands on the front thigh. Toes, knees and hips should all face forwards. Feel the stretch in the bulky part of the muscle. Hold for 10 seconds and repeat on the other side. Alternatively, try a stair stretch. Stand with the balls of the feet on the edge of the step and ease both heels down slowly. Do this gently to avoid stretching excessively. Hold the stretch for 10 seconds.

ALTERNATIVE

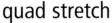

ADAPTING A QUAD STRETCH

A hip flexor stretch extends your range of movement:

- Stand in quad stretch position *(right)*
- Curl the pelvis and hip bones forwards until you feel a stretch in the front of the hip
- Hold for 5–10 seconds
- Repeat on the other side

quad stretch

Feel this stretch in the centre of the thigh. Stand with neutral pelvis and tight abs. Hold a chair or stair rail if you need support, but with practice your balance will quickly improve. Stand on the left leg and keep the knee soft. Bend the right leg behind you and reach back to grasp the right foot. Ease the foot towards the buttocks, keeping knees together and the right knee facing the floor. Breathe easily. Hold for 10 seconds, then repeat with the other leg.

abductor stretch

This is a stretch for the inner thigh. Stand with good posture, long spine, neutral pelvis, tight abs and feet slightly wider than hip-width apart. Turn the right foot out slightly and keep the left foot facing forwards. Keeping both feet flat on the floor, bend the right knee. Feel the stretch in the left inner thigh. Hold for 10 seconds. Repeat on the other side.

standing hamstring stretch

Place the right foot in front of you, with the right leg straight. Do not put any weight on it. Bend the left knee, push the hips backwards and place your hands on the left thigh. Keep your chest lifted and back straight and lean forwards from the hips. Feel the stretch in the back of the right thigh. Tighten the abdominals, then lift your right buttock upwards for a more intense stretch. Hold for 10 seconds. Breathe easily throughout. Then repeat on the other leg. Alternatively, try the lying hamstring stretch (*below*).

lying hamstring stretch

Shortened (or tight) hamstrings and hip flexors are often the reason for poor posture, restricted movement and back problems. Regular stretching helps improve all these conditions, and also increase your performance in sport, dance and everyday activities. Feel this stretch in the bulky part of your thigh.

1 Lie on the floor with both knees bent, feet flat on the floor. Raise the right leg and hold the back of the thigh with both hands. Ease the leg as close to your chest as you can, then point and flex the foot and circle the ankle.

2 Stretch the leg up, keeping the knee soft. Breathe out as you feel the stretch. Hold for 10 seconds. Lower slowly and repeat with the other leg.

lower body workout

Working the lower body requires a lot of energy, but that effort is repaid with many benefits. Energetic exercise which uses the big muscles of the legs and hips speeds up your metabolic rate long after the exercise is over. Thus a combination of strength training to accentuate and define muscles, and frequent aerobic exercise to help you lose any excess fat, can dramatically improve your shape.

MAIN LOWER BODY MUSCLE GROUPS

- **Hamstrings** at back of thighs; enable knees to bend and a straight leg to extend backwards
- **Quadriceps** at front of thighs; enable knees to extend and hips to flex
- **Gluteals** in the buttocks; pull thighs to side, rotate the legs and help raise the torso upright from a forward bend position
- **Adductors** at inner thighs; pull legs inwards
- **Abductors** at outer thighs; take legs outwards and rotate them inwards
- **Hip flexors** connect the lower spine and hip bone to top of thigh; flex the hips
- **Calf** muscles at back of lower leg; enable feet to point and heels to lift
- **Tibialis** at front of lower leg; pulls the foot up

your main aims

The challenges in this section are to lift and condition the buttocks, to create a distinct separation between the buttocks and the back of the thigh, to improve the shape and tone of the front of the thigh – particularly around the knee – and to firm and shape the inner thigh.

Take time to master each exercise, and don't expect to be proficient at them all immediately. Once learnt correctly,

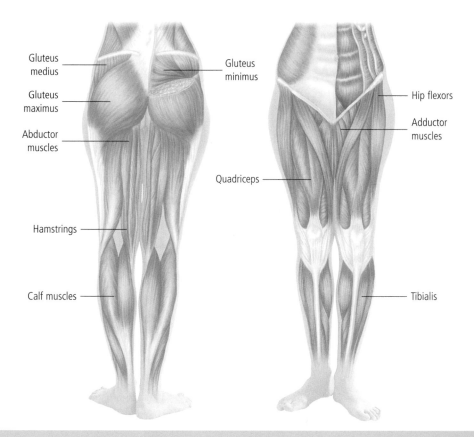

Gluteus medius

Gluteus maximus

Abductor muscles

Hamstrings

Calf muscles

Gluteus minimus

Hip flexors

Adductor muscles

Quadriceps

Tibialis

BODY TYPES

Whatever shape you want to be, your genes have determined your basic body type. Identifying your body type may help you come to terms with the difference between your desired shape and your actual shape. You may not fit perfectly into one category but tend towards one type.

Ectomorphs are long and lean; the best long-distance runners fit into this group. Mesomorphs are narrow waisted and broad shouldered, with strong hips, like sprinters and gymnasts. Endomorphs are short, with wide hips and well-rounded proportions.

they will be tools for life. Getting it right takes practice and patience. Use a mirror to check your posture and alignment through all the positions of each exercise, and if it doesn't feel right check the instructions again.

training into shape

You can move straight into this section after the warm-up. Do not pause between sections as this will diminish the fat-burning process of aerobic exercise. Muscles should be trained for both strength and stamina. Different training results in different shapes. Track athletes need power and speed

so their training includes jumping, lunging, and squatting. These moves result in finely toned, shapely buttocks and quads. Endurance runners work at a lesser intensity for longer periods and have lean frames with comparatively small musculature. Thus, to lose fat you need to do endurance training, which entails exercising at a lower intensity for longer; or to improve your shape do big, powerful moves for a shorter time. You can adapt all these exercises by changing the intensity and duration.

Rear leg raise (see p.61)

conditioned buttocks help prevent knee and back injuries

side step squat

This exercise works all the gluteals and the muscles at the sides of the hips and thighs. As this move is challenging but effective, take time to perfect it.

Use a chair the first time you do it to help you find the correct working position. Take about two seconds to step out and two seconds to step in.

1 Stand with good posture, knees soft, feet together, left foot lifted and prepared. Breathe easily throughout.

2 Step left leg wide to the side. Drop the hips down and back behind the heels while swinging the arms forwards for balance. Keep knees in line with feet and the chest lifted.

3 Step the right leg into start position, squeezing your buttocks and abs as you stand up. Start with 8, work up to 20.

side leg raise and squeeze

This demanding and effective exercise lifts and shapes the buttocks by working the deepest layers of the gluteals. Repeat five times on each leg, working up to 20 repetitions.

1 Begin in a deep squat, arms out for balance, hips low and behind heels, knees in line with feet, chest lifted and the back straight. Breathe easily.

2 Raise and rotate the left leg with the knee facing down. Pull in the arms and squeeze the buttocks and outer thigh. Return to a deep squat.

PLIÉ TIPS
- Keep the back straight as you bend the knees
- Breathe easily throughout
- Keep the upper body and hands free from tension

plié with arms

Think of strength, poise and fluidity when you do this movement. The plié has no pause, momentum or drop and, like many dance movements, it takes a lot of effort to perfect. Practise the leg movements first, then add in the arms when you are ready to do so. Repeat 10 times.

1 Position feet slightly wider than hip-width apart with legs gently turned out, arms relaxed at your sides and pelvis in neutral.

2 Keep chest lifted and ribs in line with hips as you bend the knees and take the arms out to the sides. Keep your heels down and your knees in line with your toes.

dance movements such as the plié require
great posture, alignment, strength and flexibility

3 Squeeze buttocks and quads hard as you straighten the legs and lift the arms up. Keep the knees soft, abs tight, shoulders down.

4 Bend knees deeply, smoothly bringing the arms down and out to the sides. Then straighten the legs, squeeze the buttocks and quads and bring the arms down to start position.

dip squat

Increase the challenge of this exercise by altering the timing and emphasis of the movement. For example, bend down for one count and spend three counts coming up. Try the same in reverse, or hold the position for 2–4 seconds. Use hand weights if you wish.

2 Squeeze the buttocks tight and push the hips forward as you stand up. Pull arms to the sides of the hips. Repeat 5 times, progressing to 20.

1 Squat down until the thighs are parallel to the floor, hips behind feet and with all the weight on the heels. Swing the arms in front of you for balance and momentum.

one-legged squat

The American Council on Exercise recently declared this to be the most effective bottom exercise in the world! Use a chair for support if you haven't yet mastered this tricky position.

1 Stand tall with neutral pelvis, abs tight. Place the right foot just in front of you, touching the floor. All weight should be on the rear foot.

2 Drop the hips backwards and bring your arms up for balance. Your left knee remains over the left foot. Stand up by curling the hips forward, squeezing the buttocks and pulling the arms in. Repeat 5 times on each leg, progressing to 20.

drop lunge

This exercise is demanding, working the thighs, hamstrings, hips and buttocks. Getting down and up actively, with good alignment and posture, is no easy feat. Use a chair for support to begin with, and watch out for the most common fault – of allowing the knee to slide in front of the supporting foot – by looking in a mirror. Move down and back up as cleanly as you can. Start by doing 2–4 drop lunges, about two seconds down and two seconds up, but aim for 15–20 lunges. You can, of course, go slower than this count, but not faster.

1 Take a stride forward with the left leg and place the foot flat on floor. Balance on the ball of the rear right foot. Keep the body upright, pelvis neutral and abs tight.

2 Bend knees and lower until rear knee is just off the floor. Keep back straight. To come up, push down against the front heel and squeeze the buttocks hard.

feet-together squat

This works the gluteals, quads and hamstrings. Start with 10 squats and progress to 20, about two counts down and two counts up. To add variety or intensity, descend for one count and spend three counts coming up. Try also holding the lower position for 2–4 seconds, or using hand weights.

1 Stand with good posture, feet together and knees soft. Bend the knees and drop the hips down and back behind the heels, moving the weight to the heels. Swing the arms for balance, keep the chest lifted and the back long.

2 As you stand and stretch the legs, pull arms in towards hips and squeeze buttocks hard.

buttock squeeze and stretch

This is a relatively easy exercise for the gluteals. Keep your face, neck and shoulders free from the tension you are building in your gluteals. Try to breathe easily throughout. As you squeeze, don't lift the hips too much – the emphasis is on the muscle contraction, not the height.

1 Lie on your back, hands at your sides. Keep the right foot on the floor and the right knee bent. Place the left ankle on the right knee.

2 Tighten abs and lengthen the back. Curl the hips upwards so that the buttocks lift off the floor. Squeeze the buttocks for 2–4 seconds, then carefully lower until the buttocks skim the floor for one second. Then continue: repeat 10 times on each leg.

gluteal stretch

Lie on the floor and place the left ankle on the right knee. Push the left knee outwards. Pull the right thigh towards the chest with both hands. Breathe easily. Hold for 10 counts. Repeat on the other leg.

rear leg raise

This is an adaptable exercise that works the gluteals and hamstrings. Alter the intensity by increasing the speed or using ankle weights.

1 On all fours, lean on your forearms. Stretch right leg out behind you. Tighten the abs and lengthen your spine. The hips should be above the knees, shoulders above your elbows.

2 Lift right leg, squeezing hamstrings and gluteals with more intensity as you raise your leg. Do not allow shoulders or hips to twist. Keep your back straight and control the leg movement, about two seconds up and two seconds down. Repeat 10–20 times on each leg.

shoulder stretch

Kneel and lower the hips down. Reach arms out and place forehead lightly on the floor. After a few seconds, walk the fingers further forwards to stretch a little more and relax.

inner thigh raise

This exercise quickly results in toned inner thighs. Do not allow the working leg to rest on the floor between raises, but lift it again immediately. Begin with 10 repetitions and progress to 30, about two seconds up and two seconds down.

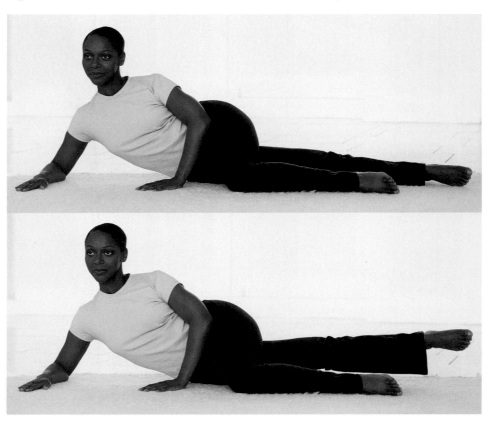

1 Lie on your right side and rest on the right elbow. Place left hand in front to help you balance. Place left knee on the floor or on a pillow in front of you. Straighten the right leg so that the inner thigh faces the ceiling. Tighten abs and check for neutral pelvis.

2 Lift and lengthen right leg, keeping knee soft. Control the movement up and down and breathe easily. Check your position and repeat.

working slowly and correctly ensures the full use of muscles

inner thigh and groin stretch

Sit on the floor. Grasp your ankles and bring the soles of the feet together. Keep your back straight and your chest lifted. Exhale and lean forwards from the hips. Hold for 5–30 seconds and relax.

outer thigh raise

This exercise works the abductors, the the muscles of the outer thigh, and the gluteals. Begin with 10 repetitions, about two seconds up and two seconds down. Make sure the leg only skims the floor before raising it again.

1 Lie on your right side, resting on the right elbow. Bend the right leg forwards to make a steady base. Straighten the top leg and turn heel upwards. Check for neutral pelvis and tighten abs.

2 Keep hips forward and raise the top leg to shoulder height. Hold for a second then lower, keeping the heel up and toes down. Begin with 10 repetitions and aim for 30. Repeat on other leg.

WHY STRETCH?

Regular stretching can improve poor posture and back problems and increase the range of movement. It enhances performance in sport and decreases the risk of injury.

standing stretch for hamstrings

Stand with good posture, feet slightly wider than hip-width apart. Place the left foot in front of you, bend the right knee and place hands on the right thigh without putting any weight on it. Push hips back. Keep the chest lifted and back straight and lean forwards from the hips. Feel a stretch in the back of the thigh. Tighten the abs and lift the left buttock for a more intense stretch. Hold for 10 seconds and repeat on the other leg.

hamstring and calf stretch

Lie with knees bent, feet on floor. Raise the left leg close to your chest, then straighten it and flex the foot. Hold for 10–30 seconds. Repeat on the other leg.

quad and hip flexor stretch

Stand on the right leg and keep the knee soft. Bend
the left leg behind you and reach back and grasp the
left foot. Ease the foot towards the buttocks, keeping
the knees together and left knee facing down to the
floor. Keep the spine long and the hips facing forwards.
Hold for 10 seconds. Repeat on the other leg.

lying quad and hip flexor stretch

Lie on your right side, resting on your right forearm.
Bend the left leg behind you and grasp the foot with
your left hand. Pull the heel towards your buttocks,
keeping your body in a straight line. Curl your pelvis
forwards and feel the stretch in your thigh and hip.
Breathe easily throughout.

lower body life activities

The activities listed below all target the big muscles of the lower body. They are cardiovascular, which means they work your heart and burn fat, and most are weight bearing, increasing bone strength and density. Look for opportunities to do these activities, even if only for short periods of time. Think of them as a bonus, a dividend for your body.

USEFUL EQUIPMENT

- Good supportive training shoes
- A bicycle
- Skipping rope
- Step box
- Mini trampoline
- Motivating music (100+ beats per minute)
- Stopwatch to record activity

fitness levels

If you want to increase your aerobic capacity and stamina, this is a good time to take up extra activities. If an activity is new to you, don't expect miracles the first time: muscles adapt only after six sessions. Also, most activities don't necessarily benefit from proficiency in other areas of fitness, hence the need to keep making new physical demands on your body. Even if you have done 10 swimming sessions this will not make your first run any easier. Apply the training principles of frequency, intensity, and duration to continue increasing your fitness.

walking and running

Walking as an exercise is not the same as wandering around the house. It can be cardiovascular if performed briskly and is a good precursor to running. I have seen great results from people who hate the idea of running by telling them to run as slowly as possible. This takes away the stress of trying to keep up with someone running at a faster pace. So relax and try to establish a rhythm that coordinates your breathing with your stride. Before a walk or run check your shoes, your route and your safety. Spend five minutes warming up and five minutes stretching and cooling down afterwards to allow your heart to adjust. Include your warm-up ankle exercises (*see p*.46). If you are unfit you need more time to warm up and cool down.

- Wear light, bright, thin layers that you can remove as you heat up. Wear cotton socks. When you cool down put clothes back on before you get cold.
- Ensure you are well-hydrated. Drink water in the hour before you exercise.
- Adopt perfect posture throughout and keep your shoulders down.
- When walking, move at a brisk pace so that after five minutes you are sweating mildly and breathing more rapidly, but still able to hold a conversation.
- Strike the ground with the heel. Push into the ground with the mid-foot to propel you forwards.
- Swing your arms to give you balance and momentum. Coordinate your stride with your breathing and arm swing.
- Keep your hands, shoulders, elbows and facial muscles free from tension.

Once you are running for 20 minutes three times a week, you will probably need better running shoes. Go to a sports shop for advice; this is also the place to inquire about running clubs.

cycling and swimming

These are both fantastic activities to do – especially if you are overweight or have problems with your joints, since they have no weight-bearing impact. For this reason, these activities have no beneficial effect on bone density. Remember that for cardiovascular training you must swim or cycle hard enough to puff lightly. Keep the exercise challenging but comfortable enough to sustain the pace.

step classes

Stepping is a vigorous exercise that improves coordination, agility, strength, stamina and cardiovascular fitness.

dance classes

Dance can mean anything from ballet to ballroom, line or tap. Dance in some form can be taken up at any age and of all cardiovascular activities, this can be the most rewarding challenge for body and mind.

trampolining

Mini trampolines, or rebounders, are fun, affordable, and small enough to have in the home. The exercise is aerobic, bone-building, good for balance and coordination and easy on joints for those with weight problems.

jumping and skipping

The main benefits of a few minutes daily of these activities is good protection against osteoporosis (*see pp*.104–105). Start by interspersing exercises from the lower body section with five skips or jumps; aim for 20 jumps or skips and repeat five times.

upper body workout

A toned upper body gives a graceful appearance to the arms, back and shoulders and generates extra power for everyday activities. Women should pay particular attention to the triceps, which make up the majority of the muscle mass in the upper arm, and which lose their definition and strength without frequent exercise.

MAIN UPPER BODY MUSCLE GROUPS

- **Deltoids** over the top of shoulders; raise the arms sideways, to the front and to the rear
- **Trapezius** across the back of the shoulders; draw shoulders together and down
- **Latissimus dorsi** stretch across the back into the arms; draw the arms down and back and rotate them
- **Pectorals** in the chest area; draw arms across the body, rotate arms inwards and support breast tissues
- **Biceps** at the front of the upper arms; enable the arms to bend and the palms to turn when the arms are bent
- **Triceps** at the back of the upper arms; straighten the elbows
- **Erector spinae** muscles keep your spine erect and enable you to bend and twist round

resistance exercise

Your muscles will quickly decline in stamina and strength unless you exercise regularly or you have a physically active job. Most women tend to be unbalanced in their body strength, with weaker arms and stronger legs, so you need to work the muscles of your upper body by doing resistance exercises using your own body weight or hand-held weights.

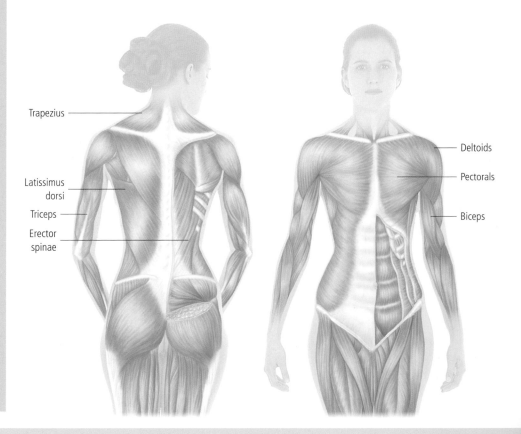

Trapezius

Latissimus dorsi

Triceps

Erector spinae

Deltoids

Pectorals

Biceps

Pectoral squeeze

using hand weights

Once you have learnt the exercises in this section you should use hand weights to continue to challenge your muscles – think of how our muscles adapt to the weight of a growing baby. The weights that you use are important to the result that you will achieve. Practise first using household items as small weights, such as cans of food or detergent bottles. Then progress onto hand-held weights. The appropriate range of weights for women to use is between one and five kilograms (2–11lbs). Whenever you use weights you must take care not to use momentum to achieve a lift. Stay in control of each movement, particularly on the downward action. A common mistake is to lean back and lock the knees or elbows, especially on the upward swing.

achieving overload

At some point you will notice that it takes longer for your muscles to tire as you exercise. This means that you are getting fitter and you will have to work harder to achieve "overload". Overload means pushing the body beyond its comfort zone. The last couple of repetitions of an exercise should be difficult, causing your muscles to ache. Your fitness will not improve until you reach this point.

well-trained muscles

Also bear in mind that your muscles will benefit from both endurance training and strengthening. The former requires less resistance work or lighter weights and more repetitions, while the latter requires you to use more resistance or choose heavier weights and perform fewer repetitions.

MUSCLE FACTS

- Muscle cannot turn to fat, nor fat to muscle; they are two different substances
- Exercises are most effective when the last few repetitions make your muscles ache
- Strength training causes an increase in muscle bulk in men because of their male hormones. However, it is very difficult for women's muscles to increase in size; they grow only when their strength is increased by about 200 per cent. Rather, women's muscles become harder, more defined, and lifted when exercised.

if you have time for only one upper body exercise, make sure it is this one

upright press-ups

These press-ups are easier to do than floor press-ups, and are one of those versatile exercises that you can do anywhere and at any time. Use a wall or a hand rail at chest height for support. To increase the intensity of the exercise, push yourself further back from the rail, or decrease the speed. Begin by doing 10 press-ups, rest and repeat; aim for 20, rest and repeat.

1 Stand one stride away from the rail. Check for neutral pelvis and tight abs. Lean body weight forward and bend the elbows.

2 Push away from the rail and straighten the arms without locking the elbows. Keep the back straight. Breathe normally.

floor press-ups

These press-ups are the finest exercise for the upper body. They work the pectorals, which support the breasts, shoulders and triceps. The easiest way to start this exercise is on all fours, with hips in line with knees and hands underneath shoulders. Begin with 10 press-ups, repeat, and aim for 20 and repeat. Do floor press-ups every day, alternating between building up your strength and your endurance (*see box, below*).

1 Place your hands under your shoulders. Keep the elbows soft and hips in line with the knees. Your knees should be on the floor and feet crossed at the ankles. Tighten your abs and maintain neutral pelvis. Breathe normally. Depending on the intensity required, walk the hands away from the hips.

2 Bend your arms until your face almost touches the floor. Count 2 seconds down, 2 seconds up. Keep your back straight. Then push up back into start position.

STAMINA AND STRENGTH

When you want to perform press-ups to improve your stamina levels, lessen the intensity of the move by altering your position: bring the knees closer to the arms and increase the number of repetitions that you do.

When you want to work to increase your strength, walk the arms as far from the hips as you can manage, or lift the knees off the floor completely. You should make the move so difficult that you can only manage 12–20 repetitions.

lower back lifts

Many people completely ignore their back when keeping fit, and after pregnancy the back is especially weak and vulnerable to injury. Try to balance the time you spend training the abs with exercise for the back. This exercise targets the erector spinae muscles that run the length of the spine. Begin with five lifts and aim for 10. To intensify the move, hold for longer.

1 Lie face down on the floor with legs together, arms on the floor at your side, pelvis in neutral position and the spine long. Keep the feet and hips pushed into the floor.

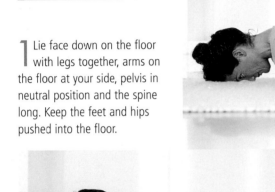

2 Keeping the neck and spine long, your head in line with the spine and your eyes down, lift your shoulders off the floor as high as possible. Hold for 2–4 seconds and lower. Breathe easily throughout.

strong back muscles help prevent backache and aid good posture

swan squeeze

This exercise is very similar to lower back lifts (*see opposite*), but adds a contraction for the upper back. Unlike the muscles at the front of the body, the back is made up of many layers of small muscles that work together to bend, twist, and lift. Upper back muscles are also often overstretched and weakened, particularly after pregnancy and breastfeeding. Repeat 5 times, aim for 10.

1 Lie face down on the floor with your legs together, arms stretched back, and pelvis in neutral. Lengthen the neck and spine. Lift the head and shoulders and squeeze the shoulder blades together firmly. Keep the feet and hips pushed into the floor.

2 Hold the upper back contraction. Lift the chest and shoulders slightly, keeping the eyes down. Maintain pelvic contact with the floor. Hold the position for 2–4 seconds and lower. Breathe easily throughout.

triceps dips

High on the list of most effective exercises, triceps dips work the shoulders and triceps – the muscles that make up most of the muscle mass in the upper arms. They must become a permanent fixture in your exercise regime if you want toned upper arms. You can do these exercises anywhere.

1 Sit on the floor, knees bent and feet parallel and flat on the floor. Place both hands behind the hips, fingers facing forwards. Bend the elbows, keeping them slightly soft.

2 Straighten arms, lifting hips off the floor. Bend elbows until your buttocks skim the floor, then straighten the arms again. Move only the arms, not the hips. Repeat several times.

bicep curl

Use weights for this movement, which isolates and works the bicep muscle only. Be precise about what you are working and what should be moving.

Do not sway at the hips or twist or bend at the waist. Maintain soft elbows and soft knees. Don't rely on momentum to help you lift your hand weights.

1 Stand with feet hip-width apart, knees soft, neutral pelvis and strong abs. Lift chest, keep shoulders down, arms at sides.

2 Hold the weights so that your palms face forward. Bend one elbow and bring the weight to your shoulder.

3 Begin to lower the arm down, keeping the elbows tucked into the body. Repeat 10 times on each arm; aim for 30 repeats.

ALTERNATIVE DELTOID RAISES

- Using the same one-joint action, try deltoid raises to the front, from thigh to shoulder, palms face down
- Or try rear deltoid raises to the rear, from hips to near shoulder level, palms face down

deltoid raises

The deltoids sit on top of each shoulder like epaulettes (*see p.68*). This exercise, which should be done with weights, shows improved shoulder definition after three or four sessions. To perform it accurately, move the arms in one motion from the shoulders, not the elbows. Your arms move from hip to shoulder level, palms facing down. Feel the work in the deltoid, not the triceps. Check your movement in a mirror: nothing else should move. Start with 10 raises and aim for 20, about two seconds up and two seconds down.

1 Stand with feet hip-width apart, knees soft, neutral pelvis and strong abs. Lift the chest. Keep shoulders down and back, arms by sides.

2 This is a one-joint action: keeping the elbows soft, raise the arms sideways and upwards from hip to shoulder height, palms facing down. Then lower the arms and repeat.

shoulder press

This exercise works the shoulders, triceps and upper back. Take extra care to keep the back straight as you push up. Begin with 10 weight lifts, about two seconds up and two seconds down, and aim for 30. To intensify the exercise, decrease the speed.

always aim for quality, not quantity

WARNING!

Whenever you use weights, you must be sure of your technique. Remember, do not swing the weights or use momentum to help you lift. Aim for control, not speed, at all times.

1 Stand with feet hip-width apart, knees soft, neutral pelvis and strong abs. Lift the chest. Hold the weights just in front of your shoulders.

2 Push up the arms smoothly. Ensure that the elbows stay soft and just the arms move. Bring the arms down with control and repeat.

never force or bounce a stretch

STRETCHING

- Being flexible enables us to reach, twist, bend and turn with ease, making everyday tasks easier
- After exercise muscles are shorter and tight. Stretching helps realign muscle length
- Take each joint slowly through its full range of movement

triceps stretch

Stand, or sit comfortably on the floor with legs crossed. Tighten the abdominals, lift your chest and maintain neutral pelvis and a long spine. Lift your right arm to the ceiling and bend the elbow, reaching your right hand down towards the shoulder blades. Hold the right elbow with your left hand and ease the elbow gently backwards, behind the head and downwards. Hold the stretch for 10–30 seconds. Breathe easily throughout. Then repeat on the other arm.

upper body stretches

Release tension in the shoulders, neck and upper back and recharge with this combination of upper body stretches. After stretching, shrug your shoulders then shake out your elbows and hands. Focus on the feeling of heaviness. Finally, drop your chin down to your chest to allow the neck to relax.

1 Stand with good posture. Raise arms up and take them back slightly behind the ears. Hold for 10–15 seconds.

2 Push your arms out in front, as far away as possible, with your palms facing away from you. Drop your chin to your chest. Hold for 10–15 seconds.

3 Pull arms back to lift, stretch and open the chest. Hold for 10–15 seconds. Repeat, moving smoothly from one move to the next. Breathe easily throughout.

abdominal exercises

Building strength and endurance in the trunk muscles is vital in order to achieve good posture and ensure that you have a strong, well-protected back. For your abdominals to have visible definition, you need trained muscles and low body fat, while achieving a flatter stomach requires building stamina in the transversus.

ABDOMINAL MUSCLE GROUPS

- **Rectus abdominus** runs from the pubic bone to the ribs and has three fibrous bands of muscle crossing it. These are what form a "six pack" shape. It curls the trunk upwards and gives support to lumbar spine
- **Transversus abdominus** is the deepest of the abdominal muscles. It lies horizontally across the trunk from the lower back round to the middle of the stomach. It stabilizes the pelvis and lower back and flattens the abdominal area
- **Internal and external obliques** sit on top of the transversus muscle and run from the hips and pelvis to the ribs. They enable the body to flex, rotate and bend to either side

support system

The abdominals act as a support system working to stabilize movements such as bending, twisting and lifting. Conditioned abdominals relieve stress on the lower back and support the internal organs. If the abdominals (the rectus, the obliques and the transversus muscles) are weak, the pelvis sags back, leading to excessive spinal curvature. This throws the whole spine out of alignment as the upper body slumps forward. The key to strengthening the abdominals, instantly improving your posture and relieving lower back pain is to practise a neutral pelvis or pelvic tilt position and compress the abs.

neutral pelvis

This is a small, subtle movement that maintains the curves of the spine but brings the pelvis forwards and the spine into alignment (*see p.*18).

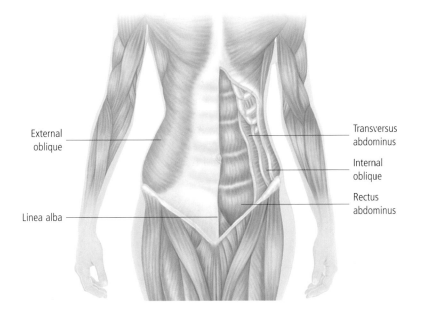

External oblique

Linea alba

Transversus abdominus

Internal oblique

Rectus abdominus

Plank level 1 (see p.88)

Level 2 of Plank (see p.88) strengthens the trunk muscles intensively

compressions

It is the transversus muscle that helps you pull your stomach in as if trying to attach your navel to your spine. You should be able to hold a compression for five seconds while breathing normally. Gradually increase the duration until you can hold your abdominals flat all day long, as dancers do. (*See also pp*.24–25.)

working correctly

You may be used to doing abdominal crunches without pulling the muscles flat first. If so, you will wonder why your stomach is not flat even though it may be fit from you working the rectus muscles. Performing 100 crunches

without compressing the transversus muscle first will not result in a flat stomach. The natural urge when performing a crunch is for the rectus abdominus muscle to "dome" upwards, so making the action easier. Only the transversus can stop this doming by pulling all the muscles flat. This correct way of working requires twice the effort but does achieve the right results.

Meanwhile, the muscles that accentuate the waist, the obliques, are strengthened by twisting and rotating with a crunch action (*see p*.83). Once you have become fully coordinated in your abdominal work you can gain satisfaction from working all three sets of abdominal muscles at once.

THE LINEA ALBA

The linea alba is a line of connective tissue that runs from the pelvis to the ribs. This muscle becomes elastic during pregnancy due to the presence of the hormone relaxin in the body. After childbirth it is important to regain strength in the rectus and transversus muscles first before doing any abdominal work that involves a twisting action since twisting works the obliques, which are attached to the linea alba.

basic crunch

Take time to learn this exercise correctly since you will probably be doing it for the rest of your life! You can intensify the movement by working at half speed. Avoid resting when you lower your upper back, shoulders and head down; just skim the floor and lift up again. Do not pull on the neck as you lift your upper body. Begin with 10 repetitions, one or two seconds up, one or two seconds down and aim for 25 repetitions.

CRUNCH TIPS

- Exhale as you lift up and inhale on the way down
- Avoid straight leg sit-ups and traditional full sit-ups. They put the back at risk and are less effective for the abs than crunches

1 Lie on the floor with knees bent, feet flat and hip-width apart. Keep the knees a comfortable distance from your buttocks. Keep the shoulders relaxed and down. Support your head with your hands. Keep pelvis in neutral and your abs pulled flat as you inhale.

2 Compress the abs and exhale as you lift your head, shoulders and ribs off the floor. Lift as high as you can, keeping the lower back on the floor, the hips still and the abs pulled flat. Lower and inhale.

crunch twist

This is a variation on the basic crunch, using the rectus abdominus, transversus abdominus and oblique muscles. The crunch twist is another exercise that you will be doing for the rest of your life, so spend time perfecting your form. To intensify the workout, reach for your outer thigh, work at half speed, or hold the uppermost position for two seconds. Begin with 10 repetitions, one or two seconds up, one or two seconds down, and aim for 30 repetitions.

1 Lie with knees bent, feet flat and hip-width apart. Keep knees a comfortable distance from the buttocks, and shoulders relaxed and down. Support head with left hand. Keep pelvis in neutral and abs compressed. Inhale, lift head and shoulders as high as possible, exhale, twist from the waist, and reach to the left knee with your right hand.

2 Bring your right hand back behind your head as you return to start position. Keep the abs flat as you inhale. Repeat on the other side, reaching out with your left hand as you twist your torso at the waist. The lower back stays in contact with the floor.

FLOOR WORK

- Use a supportive mat for these exercises
- Avoid the swinging and bouncing that often – wrongly – accompany these exercises, and you will see exactly how much muscle control you have
- Don't hold your breath during strenuous work; it makes your job harder and raises blood pressure
- Practise slow, steady breathing, inhaling as you prepare and exhaling as you exert the effort

reverse curl level one

This is a superb exercise if performed correctly. Use the power of your muscles, not momentum, to curl the pelvis towards the ribs and lift and lower the body smoothly. Begin with 10 repetitions, one or two seconds up, one or two seconds down, and aim for 20 repetitions.

1 Lie on the floor, knees bent into chest, ankles crossed, arms by your sides, palms down. The legs should feel completely relaxed. Your arms may assist the action by lightly pushing down on the floor.

2 Compress abs. Curl the spine upwards and the pelvis towards the ribs. As you exhale work the abs. Lift hips, relax shoulders, arms and face muscles. Inhale as you lower.

reverse curl level two

This is a harder version of the reverse curl. For this, keep your arms behind your head. Make the movement small and focus on the upwards motion rather than forwards and back. Don't let your feet swing back and forth. Begin with 10 repetitions, one to two seconds up, one to two seconds down; aim for 20 repetitions.

1 Lie on the floor, knees bent into chest. The legs should feel completely relaxed. Cross your ankles and support your head with your hands.

2 Compress abs and curl the spine upwards and the pelvis towards ribs as you exhale. Inhale as you carefully lower the hips.

double crunch level one

Here both ends of the rectus abdominus muscle lift upwards (and the spine curls up, too) making a "c" shape. This exercise requires skill, strength and stamina. Avoid using momentum to achieve the lift. Begin with 10 repetitions, one or two seconds up, one or two seconds down; aim for 20.

1 Lie on the floor, knees bent into chest, ankles crossed. The legs should feel completely relaxed. Support head with hands. Compress abs and inhale.

2 Exhale and use your abs to lift your head and shoulders off the floor and to curl the pelvis slowly towards the ribs. Lower smoothly and inhale.

double crunch level two

This is an extremely demanding exercise. The legs are unsupported, so you need strong enough abdominals to hold the body in position while completing the lift. The legs must be far enough over the torso to avoid stressing the back. Begin with five repetitions, one to two seconds up, one to two seconds down; aim for 20 repetitions.

1 Raise both legs, keeping knees bent and ankles crossed. Support head with hands. Your legs will stay in this position throughout.

2 Compress abs. Exhale and lift head, shoulders, ribs and pelvis off the floor. Hold the lift at the top for 2 seconds, then lower.

killer curl

This is truly demanding. Each stage of the exercise needs to be clearly defined and mastered. Check that you have flat abdominals and a neutral pelvis as you learn each position. Relax the face, hands and shoulders and breathe easily throughout. The sequence takes 40–60 seconds. Repeat 1–5 times.

1 Lie on your back on the floor, arms at your sides, feet flat and knees bent. Check for neutral position.

2 Lift up your chest and shoulders and hold on to the backs of the thighs. Pause for a few seconds to check the abs are flat. Breathe normally.

3 Walk your hands up to the backs of the knees. Using your arms for support, lift your upper body up high, pause, enjoy the stretch through the back, then lower down just enough so that the lower back is in contact with the floor.

enjoy the feel of the flexibility of the spine and the power of your abdominals

4 Maintain the position but take your hands away from your legs. Reach forward with your arms 8–16 times. It will get more and more difficult to maintain flat abs, so keep checking.

5 Compress the abdominals one last time. Slowly uncurl towards the floor. Stay in control all the way.

6 Return to start position, lying flat on your back with your arms at your sides.

the plank encourages your trunk muscles to increase in strength and stamina

the plank level one

This yoga exercise targets the rectus abdominus, transversus abdominus, the obliques and the erector spinae – all postural stabilizers. It is a demanding movement that requires patience and skill. There are two levels of intensity: aim to hold level one for 10–30 seconds, then relax and repeat.

1 Lie face down on the floor. Lean on your forearms and look down. Compress the abs and relax the buttocks.

2 Lift your stomach and hips off the floor and hold. Lengthen the neck and spine and aim to make a straight line from shoulder to knee. There should be no movement apart from your breathing.

the plank level two

Level two of the plank further increases your stamina and strength as you hold the position for longer – 10–60 seconds – while keeping your knees off the floor. Relax, then repeat. Breathe easily throughout.

1 Lie face down on the floor. Lean on your forearms and look down. Compress the abs and check for neutral spine.

2 Lift the stomach, hips and knees off the floor and balance on the balls of the feet. Hold and breathe easily. Lengthen neck and spine and aim for a straight line between heels and shoulders, with the weight evenly distributed between forearms and feet.

complete back stretch

Always finish abdominal work with a complete back stretch to realign the muscles. Lie on your back and bring the knees into the chest. Exhale, then lift your head and shoulders towards the knees. Feel the stretch in your back – enjoy and hold for 10–20 seconds – then release. Repeat when you need to release back tension or to relieve aches.

complete neck stretch

You will need to relax and stretch your neck after abdominal work. Before you start, sit or stand comfortably, check that your spine is long, your chest is lifted, and that your shoulders are down and back and level with each other. Repeat when you need to stretch out or release back tension.

these simple stretches take seconds but release hours of tension

1 Start with a long neck, as though your head is held up by a piece of string. Look to the right slowly. Pause.

2 Breathing deeply and evenly, look slowly round to the left, as far as is comfortable. Pause again.

3 Move chin to chest and hold for 10–20 seconds. Slowly drop down through the centre to the other shoulder, making a semicircle.

stretching and relaxing

Two types of stretching technique are explored in this book. Preparatory stretches maintain or realign muscle length, while developmental stretches increase muscle length. Learning where the muscles are and what they do can help you to focus on improving any inflexible areas and to relax, making stretching more satisfying.

FOCUS ON STRETCHING

- Stretch daily – perhaps as you watch TV or relax
- Short stretches maintain muscle length; long stretches increase muscle length
- Spend time stretching the more inflexible parts of your body

---

preparatory stretching

Why stretch? Initially we stretch as part of a warm-up. When athletes or gymnasts warm up, they prepare their bodies for maximum activity. These preparatory stretches ensure that all joints, limbs and muscles have been carefully taken through their full range of movement and as a result will not be shocked and damaged when utilized during the competition or performance. The same rules apply to our own exercise programmes.

All the stretches illustrated so far in this book have been preparatory or maintenance stretches. These moves are usually held for between 10 and 15 seconds.

developmental stretching

Developmental stretches cause muscles to lengthen, so increasing an individual's range of movement and improving posture. These stretches are held for longer and are best performed on the floor because it is easier for your muscles to relax and stretch in this situation. Muscles will also stretch more easily when warmed and pliable. Developmental stretches are held for between 15 and 60 seconds.

improving your flexibility

Flexibility is often only fully appreciated when our normal range of movement is lost or suspended due to illness or injury. Only then do we

Lying gluteal stretch

realize how important it is to be able to reach, bend and twist easily to perform our daily tasks. You may also notice how even standing correctly requires strength, flexibility and balance in all the muscles. This sort of experience gives us a glimpse of what happens as we age. Muscles are adaptable and so become shorter over time as part of the ageing process and in response to daily demands. Unfortunately, many postural problems creep up on us and we may not even be aware of our bad habits until something major crops up.

Developmental stretches can correct the alignment of all the postural muscles – especially necessary if you spend much of your day sitting, driving or typing, or if you are inflexible due to an illness or injury. As well as increasing the length of muscles, developmental stretches can help to balance the strength of those muscles that work in opposition to each other, such as the quadriceps and hamstrings or the chest and upper back muscles.

stretching to relax

Preparatory and developmental stretches also release muscle tension. Stress and injury can cause muscle spasms, while mental stress often causes muscular tension, particularly in the neck and shoulders. Your muscles will get tighter and more bunched unless you release tautness by stretching calmly and slowly. Use appropriate music or silence to help you to feel calm and relaxed. Focus on the feeling of release in the muscles. Breathe deeply and, as you breathe out, imagine the tension dropping away into the floor.

Sitting gluteal stretch

HOLDING A STRETCH

The effects of relaxin, the pregnancy hormone that causes a softening of the ligaments in preparation for childbirth, may remain in the body for up to five months after the delivery, thus making joints unstable. For this reason only preparatory stretches should be practised during the postnatal period, and these should be held for 5–10 seconds only.

High-impact activities are also best avoided during this time, especially sports such as squash, tennis and skiing – or any activity that requires fast, explosive movements where the joints cannot be carefully and properly positioned first.

Developmental stretching (held for 15–60 seconds) should only begin at least 4–5 months after childbirth.

lying hamstring stretch

Having flexible hamstrings enables you to undertake a greater range of safe movement without the risk of back injury. This exercise gently stretches all the muscles down the back of the legs, and should feel good. Ease into the stretch, and as you breathe out focus on relaxing the muscles. Hold and then stretch a little further. Try to release all tension from the muscle.

1 Keeping your left foot on the floor, lift the right leg up. Hold on to the back of the thigh, then move your hands up the leg and get a good grip around your calf. Stretch your leg out and breathe in.

2 Exhale, pulling the leg towards you. Pause, then pull in further. Hold for between 15 and 60 seconds. Repeat on other leg.

keep all your stretch movements smooth and controlled

hip, spine and shoulder twist

Lie on your back, bend the right knee into your chest, take it across your body, and place it on the floor (you may want to place a pillow under your knee). Take your arms out to the sides and look towards your right hand. Breathe deeply and ease your right shoulder into the floor. Hold for up to 60 seconds, then repeat on the other side. Feel this stretch in the middle and lower back, then, as the muscles relax, in the upper back.

quadricep and hip flexor stretch

This is another stretch to take time over. Lie on your left side with your head on your outstretched arm. Bend the right leg behind you and grasp hold of the foot. Keep your body in a straight line and pull the heel towards the buttocks. As you breathe out, curl the hips forwards to feel the stretch in the hip. Hold the stretch for up to 60 seconds, then repeat on the other side.

cat stretch

This is a simple and enjoyable back stretch to do any time to relieve tension. You can even do this movement without a warm-up.

1 Begin on all fours with neutral pelvis and tight abs. Lengthen your neck and spine.

2 Compress the abs, curl your pelvis forwards, and bring your chin to your chest. Pull the area between your shoulder blades up to the ceiling; accentuate the curve as far as you can. Hold for up to 60 seconds.

back and shoulder stretch

Move your weight back until the buttocks are above the heels and the forehead rests on the floor. Reach the right hand forwards and pause. As you breathe out, gently push the right shoulder towards the floor. Relax into the stretch. Repeat on the other side.

ease slowly
in and out
of a stretch

inner thigh stretch

Sit tall. Bring the soles of the feet together. Keeping your spine long, your chest lifted and your shoulders down, push your knees towards the floor. Hold the stretch for 15–60 seconds. For a more intense stretch, keep your knees down, hold your ankles and stretch forwards from the hips.

inner thigh and hamstring stretch

The most difficult thing about this stretch is keeping your back straight at the same time as you rotate the legs at the hip. Common mistakes include rounding the back and allowing the knees to roll forwards. Of all the stretches mentioned, this is probably the most difficult to perfect.

1 Sit tall with a long spine, chest lifted, legs apart and knees slightly bent and facing the ceiling. Put your hands on the floor in front of you to stabilize you. Breathe deeply. As you exhale, stretch forwards from your hips.

2 To increase the stretch, straighten the legs, but check that the knees are still facing up. As you lean forwards onto your hands you will have to work harder to keep your back straight.

seated side stretch

You should feel a continuous stretch from the fingertips through to the hips in this exercise. If you put the soles of your feet together you will also get a good stretch in the groin, but you may find it more comfortable to cross your legs. Sit tall with your chest lifted and shoulders down, and breathe easily.

ease into the stretch and breathe deeply; as you relax your muscles, imagine butter melting

1 Sit with feet together and, with the right hand on the floor to stabilize you, reach your left arm up overhead.

2 Tighten the abs and lean to the right side, keeping the buttocks on the floor. Hold for up to 60 seconds and repeat on the other side.

upper back stretch

I love this stretch as it isolates the upper back area and releases tension. Feel the muscles relax on the exhale and your energy levels rising on the inhale. Bring the soles of the feet together or cross the ankles. Drop the chin, clasp the hands and push the arms away from the body, curling your back. Lean back gently and hold the stretch for 15–30 seconds.

POSTURE

Check how good your postural muscles are by sitting upright on a stool with your feet on the floor. If your posture is good, the space between your shoulder blades will be 10–16cm (4–6in). See how long you can maintain the position. If you sit for much of the day, you should train to do this well. Sit upright on a stool for a little longer every day.

deltoid stretch

Stand straight, feet hip-width apart and knees soft. Raise your right arm to chest height. Keep the arm long, but with the elbow soft. Push your arm firmly backwards with your left hand until you feel the stretch around the shoulder. Hold for 10 seconds and repeat on the other side. Breathe deeply and evenly throughout.

do not continue with a stretch if you feel pain

triceps stretch

Raise your right arm to chest height and bend it in front of your body so that your right palm rests by your left shoulder. Push the upper arm towards your chest with the left hand until you feel a good stretch. Hold for 10 seconds and repeat on the other arm. Breathe deeply and evenly as you stretch.

swan stretch

Sit on the floor. Bend your knees keeping your feet flat on the floor in front of you. Walk your hands behind you, with your fingers pointed away from your body. Lift your rib cage up, press your chest forwards and pull your shoulders back. Look up slightly and enjoy the stretch in your chest, shoulders and arms. Hold for 30–60 seconds and breathe deeply.

seated back release

This helps ease tension, stretches the back and aids circulation. Sit cross-legged, or bring the soles of your feet together. Use your hands for support and relax your head and upper back forwards. As the muscles release, drop lower. Breathe deeply. Feel the stretch from the neck down the spine to the buttocks. Hold for 30–60 seconds.

03

NUTRITION

Most of us begin to make choices about what we eat and how we live when we are in our late teens. This period, until middle adulthood, is often when we are at our most complacent about – and sometimes even abusive of – our health. What we eat and drink, and what we do or don't do with our bodies, will affect us in the short and the long term. We need to establish optimal health for all the family, from pregnancy onwards, and maintain it throughout our lives.

breastfeeding and nutrition

Most pregnant women hope to breastfeed their baby after the birth, and while you don't need to eat for two while you are breastfeeding, you should think twice as hard about your nutrition. During the first months of your baby's life you should eat good food and get plenty of sleep over and above anything else. Be patient with your body, and aim to put back what your baby has taken out.

BREASTFEEDING AND EXERCISING

- Avoid vigorous exercise until at least six weeks after the birth of your baby and until you are confident of a consistent milk supply
- Before exercising, empty your breasts of milk since vigorous arm movements may set off the milk flow
- Avoid gym work in the first two months after childbirth since the risk of joint injury is high when performing resistance work
- Swimming is beneficial: the joints, breasts and pelvic floor are all supported by the buoyancy of the water
- Avoid the leg action in the breaststroke: it can stress the joint at the front of the pelvis, which is vulnerable during the postnatal period
- If you join an aqua aerobics class, keep your chest underwater as the breasts pull heavily when you move

meeting your own needs

To ensure the production of an ample, healthy milk supply, breastfeeding mothers need an extra 500 calories a day (unless overweight to start with), should drink more (non-caffeinated) fluids and take extra calcium. The normal recommended daily intake of calcium is 700–800mg, but this rises to 1,250mg while breastfeeding – equivalent to two pints of skimmed milk or four 200g yoghurts, for example.

Ideally, your nutrients should come from food, but unless you can be sure that your diet is nutritionally complete it is better to take a supplement than go without (see p.113). Remember to eat a good quality, balanced diet.

your milk supply

While you breastfeed you should not put on weight, but if you lose weight rapidly you may not be eating enough. The more often you breastfeed your baby and the more vigorously she feeds, the more milk you are likely to have. Being worn out or upset can affect how much milk you produce for your baby, and be aware that running around may impair your ability to breastfeed

successfully. Avoid vigorous exercise since it can affect the quality and quantity of your milk, and if you have an option on being busy, don't be.

Have a drink every time you breast-feed in addition to what you normally drink. Water is best, although fruit teas, juices, thin soup or stock, or skimmed milk are suitable. Avoid or limit caffeine as too much will upset a baby. If your urine becomes very dark, you should increase your fluid intake.

foods to avoid

If you or your family have no food allergies, then most foods that you eat won't cause your baby problems. If there is an allergy in the family, some foods might adversely affect your baby, causing colic, eczema, or wheezing. Cow's milk is a common offender, as are citrus fruits, tomatoes, eggs, wheat, and peanuts. It takes an estimated four to six hours from the time you eat food for it to affect your milk. You can establish any relationship between certain foods that you have eaten and a reaction in your baby by keeping a written record for a few weeks or so.

a vegetarian diet

If you have a meat-free diet, ensure that you get enough calories, protein, vitamins and minerals, such as iron and calcium, each day. This means being particularly aware of your food choices and the importance of eating a variety of plant food proteins during the course of the day. (*For more information, see pp.114–115.*)

giving up breastfeeding

If you are returning to work, or want to give up breastfeeding, try to feed your baby for at least the first 12–16 weeks so that she can benefit from the protective qualities of the milk. We know that this is the ultimate food to nourish our babies, but breastfeeding is impossible for some and difficult or impractical for others. I don't know any woman who feels nonchalant if breastfeeding is proving problematic. I breastfed my first baby for a year, but my second baby was ravenous before I had to accept that he, and I, just couldn't do it. In these situations we must thank our lucky stars for formula milk and start to see the funny side of life again.

BREAST SUPPORT

The breasts are made up of soft tissue and fat, and held in place by ligaments. After conception, pregnancy hormones begin to deposit fat cells and milk cells in the breasts, so to avoid stretching these ligaments the breasts need constant support during pregnancy and breastfeeding, and extra support when you exercise during the postnatal period.

Sports bras are more comfortable than feeding bras, and being elastic they grow and shrink with your breast size. If you need to, wear two sports bras with the largest on top. Ensure they are not too tight or the resulting pressure may block milk ducts. Also wear a sports bra under a swimming costume when you swim to prevent the breasts dragging in the water.

strong bone health

From the age of about 35 onwards, women's bones slowly lose bone mineral density (BMD). After the menopause, women's BMD decreases further as levels of oestrogen, which protects the skeleton, are much lower. As bones become less dense and more fragile and porous, they become brittle and can easily fracture or break. Most of the broken hips experienced by older people are caused by BMD loss. However, a poorly balanced diet and inactive lifestyle can result in much younger women suffering, too.

RISK FACTORS FOR OSTEOPOROSIS

- Low levels of oestrogen. Levels fall during severe dieting, the menopause, or after surgical removal of or damage to the ovaries
- Small, slight women are more at risk as they have less bone mineral density
- If a member of your family has brittle bones then you are more at risk
- An inadequate intake of calcium, especially in adolescence
- Being underweight and/or having an eating disorder that leads to missed periods
- Conditions, such as coeliac disease, that affect how well the bowel absorbs nutrients
- Long-term use of medications such as corticosteroids
- An inactive lifestyle
- Smoking or heavy drinking
- Thyroid disease

bone-building health

Osteoporosis is part of the ageing process that affects more women than men, partly because they have smaller bones that contain fewer minerals and partly because of the natural decline of oestrogen levels. One in three women develops osteoporosis. By the age of 65, the average woman has lost 26 per cent of her BMD, whilst the average man has lost just nine per cent. Calcium is the major constituent of bones and teeth, and an adequate intake is vital

throughout your lifetime. Ideally, you should get your calcium needs from food, but it is better to take a calcium supplement combined with magnesium – which is also involved in the formation of bone – than no calcium at all. The best sources of calcium are milk, cheese and yoghurt, poppy and sesame seeds, almonds, figs, Brazil nuts, muesli, tofu, white chocolate, soya haricot and green beans, sardines and whitebait (if the bones are eaten), as well as dark green leafy vegetables – especially kale, broccoli, and spring greens – eaten lightly boiled. The finest way to include bone-building calcium and magnesium in your diet is to eat muesli with sunflower and sesame seeds, Brazil nuts, hazelnuts and milk. Eating at least five portions of fruit and vegetables a day also protects bone health.

Vitamin D is needed by the body for the proper absorption of calcium. It is generated in the skin from gentle and regular exposure to sunlight, and is also found in oily fish, liver, eggs and fortified foods.

building bone strength

Osteoporosis can be prevented or actually reversed by doing weight-bearing exercise: bones are alive and must be challenged daily. Just as your muscles increase in strength and mass with exercise, so bones become stronger and denser when "loaded". The normal loading of the skeleton is the pull of your working muscles on your bones and the pull of gravity.

To counteract the effects of ageing you need to work the bones more as you grow older. More than three days of bed rest will decrease bone density in the same way as would the same amount of time spent in space or water. Swimming and cycling, whilst being beneficial in other ways, do not generate the necessary pull of gravity on the skeleton.

So keep it short and high-impact and vary the movement. One minute of jumping, skipping, stair climbing, running, or dancing every day is all that is needed; jumping for seven minutes once a week does not give the same results. Only 50 loadings a day are necessary. Your bones need this action forever, not just after Christmas!

if you have brittle bones

These directions are intended for healthy pre-menopausal women. If you think you have brittle bones, then the movements I've outlined above are not appropriate. Talk with your doctor if you think you are at risk. Diagnosis is made with a bone scan and an exercise prescription should be given to you, focusing on non-impact strengthening work and improving your balance.

eating a balanced diet

Fats provide the body with energy and the fat-soluble vitamins A, D, E and K, as well as essential fatty acids that cannot be made by the body. But eating too much of the wrong type of fats, such as saturated and hydrogenated or trans-fats, could fur up the arteries and cause heart disease. So remember these fat facts and improve your diet!

THE LOW-DOWN

- Fat contains the most calories, per gram, of any food we eat, and we need to be aware of this if we are to eat a balanced diet for a healthy lifestyle. See the comparisons below on how food types compare:
- 1 gram of fat provides 9 calories
- 1 gram of protein provides 4 calories
- 1 gram of sugar provides 4 calories
- 1 gram of alcohol provides 7 calories

fat facts

Fat cells in the body develop in early childhood; the number and distribution of fat cells you have depends on your genetic make-up. Fat cells are like a balloon: the more fat in a cell, the larger it will become. If you lose fat, the fat cell decreases in size. Once full, more fat cells can develop. This helps to explain why people always put on weight in the same place.

Once protein and carbohydrates are consumed, they are broken down and sent to wherever they are needed in the body. Only when all functions have been fulfilled will excess energy be converted to fat. The unique thing about dietary fat is that it does not go anywhere else first. The fat you consume goes directly to fat cells before being used. If we take in more calories than we burn, then more fat is stored than used and we gain weight (and vice versa for weight loss).

good fats, bad fats

Fats such as polyunsaturated and monounsaturated fats can be beneficial to the body. Too many saturated fats, found mainly in dairy and animal produce, boost "bad" cholesterol in the bloodstream, which can clog the arteries and lead to heart disease. These fats, which are hard at room temperature, should be limited. There is also another type of fat, which is man-made and called trans-fat or hydrogenated fat. These are cheap and frequently used in the manufacture of margarines, biscuits and cakes (*see opposite*).

Two types of polyunsaturated fats – omega 3 and omega 6 – are known as essential fatty acids. These are needed by the body to function effectively. Omega 3 is found in oily fish – salmon, mackerel, sardines, whitebait, herrings and kippers – linseeds, soya beans, rapeseed oil, wheatgerm and walnuts. Most of us would benefit from more omega 3 oils, and unless you eat oily fish once or twice per week consider taking a fish oil capsule daily. Omega 6 is found in sunflower seeds, safflower seeds, corn, pumpkin seeds, sesame seeds, hemp seed oil, evening primrose oil, and borage oil.

Olive oil, rapeseed oil, groundnut oil and avocados contain monounsaturated fats. Research has shown that these fats boost good cholesterol and lower bad cholesterol, especially when used in place of saturated fat. In Mediterranean countries the high olive oil intake is generally considered to be one reason for less cancer and heart disease.

the hidden dangers

Many of us don't realize that healthy fats can become unhealthy when they are heated; heated and processed fats oxidize rapidly and generate free radicals in the body, making them an unnatural and potentially harmful food.

Unsaturated fats can be chemically converted to a less healthy type of fat, known as trans-fat. It is usually found in products where hydrogenated or partially hydrogenated oils are listed on the ingredients label.

In margarine, for example, vegetable oil is hydrogenated to make it solid or semi-solid. Trans-fats are a by-product of this process. Trans-fats are of no use to the human body. They may raise cholesterol levels and block the body's

ability to process healthy poly-unsaturated fats. Trans-fats are hidden in many manufactured foods besides margarine. Crackers, biscuits, cookies, cakes and cake mixes, crisps, pastries, children's ready-made meals, cereals, sauce mixes, peanut butter, salad dressings, mayonnaise, pizza, pies, puddings, many frozen food products, and even some wholemeal breads and crackers that purport to be healthy may all contain trans-fats.

When you want to eat these foods, make sure that they are home-made using butter, or a margarine labelled "trans-fat free", or look for brands without hydrogenated oils and fats on the label.

which fats to use

Olive oil is the best oil to fry, and a polyunsaturated oil such as sunflower, safflower, or sesame oil is best for dressings or marinades. Most

Use sesame oil as a base for a healthy salad dressing

Aim for healthy, balanced meals when you eat as a family

importantly, learn these fat facts and read the food labels of whatever you buy carefully. Food manufacturers are aware that the public knows that polyunsaturates are good, but not that they become less healthy when they are hydrogenated or made solid for use in processed foods.

the dieting world

In view of the fact that many of us now eat too much of the wrong foods, a successful diet industry has emerged, inventing new diets, products, diet aids, supplements, books and clubs. Diets spread almost faster than gossip. There is a diet based on blood groups and one on astrological signs, a pop-

corn diet, a pineapple diet, a cabbage diet, a grapefruit diet, a food combining diet, and a high protein diet.... Clearly many people find it easier to begin a completely different diet rather than adjust their normal intake

losing fat the healthy way

People lose weight when they take in fewer calories than they expend. So although you lose fat if you eat only cabbage, you also lose muscle and water too – at a cost to your body.

The best diet is one that you can enjoy and which doesn't deplete your body's reserves. Your diet must make nutritional sense if it is to be one that you can live with. Plan for life as opposed to the next fortnight. Make it one that you can afford, too, and which is good for other family members. It must be socially acceptable in and out of your home, and it needs to include all the necessary nutrients and fibre. Simply put, the prescription includes eating plenty of fruit and vegetables, at least five portions per day. Try to include some raw produce if possible. Base your meals on slow-release complex carbohydrates (*see p*.112–113). Eating five or six small meals a day may be better for your energy levels and metabolism than having three larger meals.

Eat more fish and reduce your intake of meat (*see p*.114–115). By getting your fats from fish, nuts, and seeds, and decreasing the amount of meat and full-fat dairy products you eat, you'll also help to reduce your risk of developing cancer, heart disease, depression, and premenstrual tension. Don't skip breakfast; instead, get your energy flowing and your metabolism moving with tea, fruit, muesli or whole-meal bread with Marmite or mashed banana. Eat little and often to regulate your appetite and remember that skipping meals almost always creates a bottomless pit of hunger. Sensible eating provides a blueprint for life, so what you buy and how you eat will have a huge influence on your family's eating habits.

make each calorie worth it

Limit your fat and sugar intake and don't waste your calories on other people's treats like dull biscuits, ice creams, crisps, and peanuts. Limit over-processed foods, too, they are a waste of calories. You only have so many calories to spend, so spend carefully. Make each calorie worth it. Exclusion zones do not work for me because once I feel deprived I don't care about being virtuous. There should be some scope for indulgence – but just ensure that whatever you eat is worth the payback!

HOW MANY CALORIES DOES YOUR BODY NEED?

The heavier you are, the more calories you need in order to maintain your weight. Likewise, the more muscle mass you have, the more calories you need to maintain it. However, the difference between fat and muscle is that muscle is metabolically active, burning up calories, whereas fat just sits there doing relatively little.

As a rough guide, a woman weighing 63kg (140lb) needs 1,400 calories a day simply to maintain her weight while staying inactive in bed. Every second of extra activity she does through the day increases the total amount of calories needed by her body for energy. Therefore, an active woman weighing 63kg (140lb) requires about 2,000 calories a day to maintain her current weight, and approximately 500 extra calories if she is breastfeeding. Since one pound of weight is equivalent to 3,500 calories, in order to lose 450 grams (1lb) of fat each week she would need to eat 1,500 calories daily (or 2,000 calories if she is breastfeeding).

Beware of any diet or weight-loss plan that promises to shed more than 900 grams (2lb) a week. These diets involve losing not just fat, but water and extra muscle, too. (*See pp.110–111 for more information on metabolism.*)

gram for gram, fat contains more than twice as many calories as carbohydrates or protein

improving your metabolism

We know that our bodies need fuel, as does a car. We can increase the performance of a car with good fuel, and we know that cheap or incorrect fuel causes unnecessary wear and tear on the engine. For us it's the same: we work better on good quality fuel and burn more fuel when going faster. Unlike cars, our bodies continue to burn energy when inactive, to power basic processes such as breathing and blood circulation.

WHY EXERCISE?

- Exercise speeds up the metabolic rate, that is the rate we burn off calories even after exercise is over
- Energy output increases during exercise
- Exercise increases the amount of muscle in your body, which burns up more energy than fat when the body is active or at rest
- Fat is lost from the whole body only when energy output exceeds input, so change your metabolism and your body composition by exercising

we become fat if we take in too much fuel and do not expend it

being active

The more activity you do, the more fuel you burn. Making a decision to be more active means a better quality of life for the future; the excess weight we have after childbirth is not inevitable and permanent, neither is a flabby stomach. We are much more in control of our bodies than we sometimes admit.

Fat loss can be achieved by restricting the number of calories you eat, but the other important factor in weight control is the amount of exercise that you do and the effect that exercise has on your metabolism. Start to regard movement and physical effort as a privilege each time you climb stairs or walk instead of drive, garden, clean, carry items, or play with children rather than watching them. The accumulation of all these small bursts of energy throughout the day will make a big difference to your total activity during a week.

the metabolic rate

Our energy output increases during exercise, but exercise also speeds up the metabolic rate at which we burn off calories for up to 24 hours after activity. Exercise also increases the amount of muscle mass in the body, and the more muscle mass you have the more calories you use up. Muscle burns up energy 24 hours a day, whereas fat is relatively inactive metabolically – it just sits there doing very little.

Genetic or medical causes of obesity are very rare. However, some people do eat large amounts and remain slim (because they burn it off) while others, particularly long-term dieters and those who are inactive, still struggle to control their weight.

weight is not an issue

Muscle is heavier and denser than fat and weighs more. Think how a lump of meat drops to the bottom of a pan and how the fat sits on top. Muscle cannot turn to fat since they are two separate types of body tissue. Muscle is an active tissue with nerves and a blood supply while fat is a relatively inert fuel store. This means that someone who has low body fat and a high proportion of muscle will use up calories faster than someone of the same weight who has more body fat and less muscle.

effective exercise

Every type of activity burns calories, but the amount burned depends on how long, how hard, and how often the activity is performed. Aerobic exercise combined with body conditioning exercises is the optimum way to achieve fat loss, increase muscular strength and endurance and improve your metabolic rate. It is a common misconception that using weights results in oversized muscles; instead of growing in size like men's muscles, women's muscles look and feel leaner and firmer as they increase in strength. The bones also become stronger and heavier with exercise, so weighing yourself without measuring your dimensions is misleading.

a fitter, stronger body

A raised metabolic rate and increased muscle mass offers more benefits, too. Exercise boosts the immune system, improves memory, regulates appetite and moods, and encourages fat loss. It gives us the ability to respond to any sudden demands made on us without causing damage to our bodies. It might be a physical demand, such as running for a bus or catching a child from a fall, or it may be a mental challenge such as working through the night to meet a deadline. Physical activity will actually keep you mentally alert and help you cope with stress and depression.

Fitness offers us the opportunity of a full life with more confidence, energy and ability. The combination of good nutrition and physical fitness and the third component, emotional balance, all makes for a better quality of life.

CRASH DIETS

If you do need to lose weight, take it slowly and avoid very low calorie crash diets. They might cause rapid weight loss, but this is mostly loss of fluid since they make the body use up its mix of glycogen (a type of carbohydrate) and fluid stores. This can lead to a 2kg (4–5lb) loss on the scales in days. Once you eat normally again, glycogen and fluid are rapidly restored and weight goes back up. Many people find they put back even more weight as they've been so deprived on their diet that they eat more than usual to make up for it. Losing a maximum of 450–900 grams (1–2lb) a week by eating wisely and being active means that most of your weight loss will be fat rather than fluid or metabolism-maintaining muscle. This healthy approach also means you're more likely to keep the weight off.

carbohydrates

Carbohydrates are complex sugars, known as starch, or simple sugars such as fructose, which is found in fruit. Simple sugars are fast-release, which means that they raise your blood sugar quickly but temporarily, but complex sugars are slow-release, providing energy for longer.

slow-release carbohydrates

WHAT TO LIMIT
- Processed white bread
- Sweets
- Biscuits
- Shop-bought cakes
- Energy bars
- Sugared cereals

Our bodies operate best on complex slow-release carbohydrates. These are vital for good brain function, consistent mood and energy levels, and for keeping hunger at bay. They are used by the body and not stored as fat since the process of converting carbohydrates into fat is much harder than turning fat into fat. They also keep you feeling fuller for longer.

Complex carbohydrates are rich in vitamins, minerals and fibre, and low in fat. This is a major advantage when trying to lose weight since starchy foods are more filling and last for much longer than the same number of calories taken as fat or sugar. Eating high-fibre foods also helps to reduce your cholesterol. Complex carbohydrates should be a base to your meals and snacks and account for half of the calories you eat – whether you need to lose weight or not.

Brown or Basmati rice are good slow-release carbohydrates, as are oats, barley, corn, buckwheat, bulgar wheat, rye bread and flour, bananas, apples, beans, lentils, new potatoes and fruit yoghurts.

Sifting flour

avoiding empty calories

Sugar is a less healthy carbohydrate. It provides the body with "empty" calories and no nutrients. The instant burst of energy it initially gives your body is followed by a slump in energy levels shortly afterwards. It is this energy slump and the accompanying hunger pangs that ruin diets. Avoid this by eating slow-release carbohydrates at mealtimes and eating healthy snacks. We would never be tempted by junk food if we always had an alternative. Watch out, too, for clever words on labels to describe sugar, such as sucrose, lactose, glucose, and maltose.

the healthy option

Eat a variety of snacks that will maintain your energy levels through the day, such as all fresh fruits – and particularly bananas to satisfy hunger pangs – dried fruit, raw nuts, seeds such as pumpkin and sunflower seeds, rice cakes, oatcakes, flapjacks, bagels, pumpernickel, breadsticks, and wholemeal bread. If you have sweet cravings, opt for carrot cake, banana bread, malt loaf, English muffins or fruit scones. For optimum nutrition, decrease your intake of fat, added sugar and alcohol and increase your daily intake of unrefined carbohydrates.

VITAMIN SUPPLEMENTS

Most of us can meet our nutritional needs with a full and varied diet. Nevertheless, busy lives mean that not everyone feels that they can eat as healthily as they would always like to. And many women don't get enough minerals such as iron (especially if they have heavy periods), selenium and magnesium in their diet. If this sounds like you, then an "insurance policy" of a one-a-day multi-vitamin and mineral supplement with amounts close to the Recommended Daily Allowances (RDAs) can be a safe and useful addition to your diet.

You may also want to consider a supplement if you are slimming, or if your diet is restricted in some way. For example, if you are allergic to dairy products and struggle to eat enough alternative calcium

sources, a daily calcium supplement is wise. Vegans need to ensure daily vitamin B12, calcium and iodine from fortified foods or supplements since animal-derived foods are the best sources of these nutrients.

Then there's the official health advice that when planning pregnancy, and for the first 12 weeks of pregnancy, women should take 400mcg of folic acid daily to help protect against neural tube defects such as spina bifida. Pregnant and breastfeeding women are also advised to take a 10mg vitamin D supplement, especially if they have limited skin exposure to sunlight (which forms vitamin D in the body). If you are pregnant, or planning pregnancy, check the suitability of any supplements – especially those with vitamin A – with your doctor or midwife.

While supplements can help prevent nutritional deficiencies, they can't replace all the health-regulating and disease-combating effects of food. Worldwide studies show that people who eat diets rich in fruits, vegetables and wholegrain cereals have much lower rates of coronary heart disease and cancer than those who don't. It seems that it's not just specific vitamins or minerals that protect our health – real food is brimming with a range of natural antioxidants and nutrients that work together to provide us with optimal nutrition for long-term health and wellbeing.

I encourage you to stay up-to-date with health news, and if you are interested in maximizing your quality of life through good nutrition, visit a qualified dietitian or nutritionist for individual advice.

protein

Protein is essential for cell growth, maintenance and repair. It is also vital for growth and development in children, and is what our muscles and our internal organs are made of. Try to ensure that the protein you eat is low in fat. In general, fish is the best low-fat source of protein, and standard dairy produce is the highest fat source.

PROTEIN FACTS

- First-class proteins are fish, lean meats, soya beans, and low-fat dairy produce
- Protein-rich foods are best eaten at breakfast and lunch; they take longer to digest and thus keep hunger at bay
- Unlike animal proteins, vegetable sources of protein are not totally digested by the body, so if you are a vegetarian eat more protein

knowing the basics

Protein is present in most foods. Even if you eat no meat or dairy produce, you can get sufficient protein from plant foods: if you are a vegan, eat soya beans, soy milk or tofu since these are the most complete plant-derived proteins. Soya beans may also help to protect women from developing breast cancer, so this is an excellent

Oily fish

and cheap food to discover. Eating more protein than you require will not build more muscle. Protein can be converted to glucose for energy if there is insufficient carbohydrate in the diet, or stored as fat if too many calories are consumed. However, fat and glucose cannot do the specialized job of protein so we must always ensure a good-quality supply. It helps to regulate our appetite, too.

high protein sources

Aim to make your protein low in fat. Meat, fish, eggs, milk, cheese and soya beans are often called first-class protein because they contain all nine essential amino acids.

Grains, nuts, seeds and pulses are sometimes referred to as second-class protein because they contain some amino acids, but not all in the optimal amounts. A variety of these foods need to be eaten through the course of the day in order for the body to be able to utilize the protein.

Do your family a huge favour and include oily fish in their diet at least once a week: the protein is plentiful and the fats found in fish protect against heart disease and stroke, and they may also help to protect against some cancers, arthritis, and depression. Sardines, herring, mackerel, pilchards, and kippers are the finest and cheapest, followed by salmon, tuna (fresh tuna contains more omega 3 than tinned tuna), and trout.

Other high sources of protein include white fish, lean meat, poultry (not the crispy, fatty skin), eggs, yoghurt and dairy products. Skimmed milk products such as cottage and curd cheese, fromage frais and yoghurt, whilst low in calories and fat, are as high in proteins and calcium as their full-fat equivalents. Soya beans, soya milk and tofu are cheap, low-fat sources of protein.

the quality of food

Limit processed meat products such as hamburgers, meat pies, hot dogs, sausages and sausage rolls – you don't need protein that badly. Make these items yourself using the leanest, best quality meat that you can afford. Organic and free range meat, milk and eggs are becoming more available, and although they are more expensive than lower quality produce, the growth in demand has lowered prices in the last decade. Organic meat is produced using traditional methods; putting animals out to graze naturally takes up valuable space and is time consuming, hence its higher cost. However, it is guaranteed free from residues of chemicals, antibiotics and hormones and tastes much better. When you consider all these factors, quality produce does not seem so expensive. We should care more about the quality of our diet.

Pulses

PROTEIN-RICH MEALS

Eating oily fish at least once a week lowers cholesterol and protects against heart disease, strokes and certain cancers. It helps to relieve the symptoms associated with arthritis and depression, and provides the body with the antioxidant selenium. For an exceptional meal, mix a muesli of oats, linseeds, pumpkin, sunflower and sesame seeds, and Brazil nuts, almonds and hazelnuts. This mix contains slow-release unrefined carbohydrates, vitamins, proteins, minerals, a little fat and anti-oxidants, which help protect against heart disease, stroke, arthritis and osteoporosis.

fruits and vegetables

An ideal diet includes at least five servings of fruits and vegetables a day. Such a diet is low in fat and high in fibre, vitamins, minerals and antioxidants, which in turn can help protect the body against conditions such as high cholesterol, heart disease, colon cancer, irritable bowel syndrome, constipation and piles.

TOP BENEFITS

- Eating a variety of fruits and vegetables several times a day helps fight against various diseases
- Your intake of antioxidants may one day be shown to influence the rate at which you age. Eat at least five portions of fruits and vegetables daily to optimize your health
- Eating lots of fruits and vegetables can even help arteries work better
- Buy fruits and vegetables in season when they are cheaper and tastier
- Wash everything well before you eat it
- Blueberries, blackberries, strawberries, plums, garlic, kale, spinach, sprouts, alfalfa sprouts and broccoli are top-scoring nutrients on the antioxidant scale. Top dried foods include cocoa powder, green tea, prunes and raisins

making dietary changes

Changing your diet to include more fruit and vegetables needs some discipline and careful forethought. If you are worried about the expense of buying so much fresh produce, then go to a market where prices are often less than half those in supermarkets. If you shop only once a week, make a plan for the week before you buy. Choose fruits that are in season and at differing stages of ripeness, and use frozen produce, too.

vitamins and minerals

Fruits and vegetables are packed full of vitamins and minerals, and the more vegetables you can eat either raw or lightly cooked, the more these nutrients will remain intact and benefit the body.

Blueberries

There are 13 vitamins and 15 minerals that are known to be necessary to keep our bodies functioning efficiently. Vitamins are needed to balance our hormones, produce energy, boost the immune system, keep skin healthy, and protect the arteries; they are vital for the brain and nervous system and may slow down the ageing process. Minerals, meanwhile, help build bones, regulate body fluids and are components of enzymes and hormones.

antioxidants

Fruits and vegetables contain many known and unknown antioxidants. Antioxidants reduce the number of damaging free radicals in the body, which everyone produces in the process of creating energy. Excess free radicals are also produced in the body by stress, pollution, smoking, poor diet, excessive sun exposure, radiation and illness. Without sufficient antioxidants in the body to absorb them they multiply and weaken the immune system by causing cell damage, which can eventually lead to cancer and other illnesses. Free radicals can also damage previously healthy polyunsaturated fats in the body, making them unusable. These fats block cells and disable their fighting capacity. Surplus cholesterol then forms the plaque that furs up arteries.

The chief antioxidants are vitamins C, E and betacarotene, the mineral selenium, and numerous phytochemicals that exist in all fruits and vegetables. These components seem to collaborate together to defend and protect the body. Scientists do not yet know which fruits and vegetables offer the most protection so eat a good variety of them, and also eat the whole fruit – not just the juice – since it contains a greater range of nutrients.

top foods to choose

Choose fresh or frozen vegetables and fruits. Canned food can count, too – tinned tomatoes provide more antioxidants than fresh. To ensure you get the most antioxidants, choose deeply coloured fruits and vegetables – the reddest peppers and the deepest green leafy vegetables – as these often contain more antioxidants than paler varieties. Red grapes and onions have more antioxidants than white ones, and blueberries contain more antioxidants than other berries. Citrus fruits have many antioxidants, and garlic is a good source. And rather than boil vegetables, microwave, steam, grill, or stir-fry them to conserve more antioxidants.

The good news is that wine is also known to contain antioxidants – red wine contains slightly more than white. This is generally thought to be one reason why the French have very low rates of heart disease. So enjoy drinking a glass of wine with your meal.

always have some fruit in your bag to give your children when you are out and about

fit for the future

Future fitness thankfully depends not on the past but on the present: there is nothing but good news for people who plan to become fitter. All of the conditions associated with growing old can be slowed down by performing appropriate exercise. So in order to live longer and lead fuller lives we must exercise regularly and improve and monitor our nutrition for the rest of our lives.

LIFE TIPS

- Exercise for half an hour every day
- Do not smoke
- Eat as much fresh fruits, vegetables, oily fish, garlic, soya beans, low-fat dairy produce, nuts and seeds as possible
- Curb your intake of animal, dairy, hydrogenated and trans-fats, and reduce your sugar consumption

the symptoms of ageing

Almost all the symptoms that we associate with ageing are actually the result of inactivity: a decrease of muscle mass, flexibility, strength and speed, a decrease in cardiovascular ability, a weakening of the bones, stiffening of the joints, and depression. All of these things do happen gradually as part of the ageing process, but they speed up rapidly if you are inactive. Muscle begins to waste after a few days of inactivity and aerobic fitness starts to decline after two weeks. After a few days of inactivity in space even extremely fit astronauts show signs of ageing. They have higher blood pressure, wasted muscles, weaker and less dense bones, and problems with their sense of balance and with breathlessness. After several weeks of weightlessness and inactivity, standing becomes uncomfortable and walking is difficult. Imagine the harm done to elderly people left inactive in bed if this type of decline is experienced in fit, young individuals.

long-term plans

The most incredible aspect of the human body is its ability to rejuvenate and adapt. Human muscle is incredibly responsive to training and it never loses this ability. For an elderly person, performing 90 minutes of exercise a week can mean the difference between independence or being bedridden. Since modern living creates numerous health problems, and inactivity occurs not just in the elderly but in us all, your future fitness is up to you. It is never too late to reap the benefits. Before you develop your future plan, identify your priorities, weaknesses,

your motivation and how much you are prepared to change. How will you avoid junk food, fast food, party food, alcohol and cigarettes? Do not imagine it will be easy, but if you believe in your goals and have a realistic plan then success is likely.

Exercise has to be enjoyable to become a habit, but it also needs to become a priority. We have to make long-term plans that work, and get used to exercising alone. So be realistic and make plans based on the feasibility of certain activities fitting into your lifestyle. You only need to exercise for half an hour a day. Assuming your life is hectic right now, you must start doing the basics on your own. For motivation and guidance, find a fitness class that has a crèche if you need one. If you can afford a personal trainer to direct and correct you, then get one at least a few times a year. If you have no one to leave your child with, walk as much as possible. Or can you go for a run, a cycle ride or a swim? If the weather is terrible, find ways to exercise indoors. Look at equipment to boost your motivation: weights, a skipping rope or a step or a rebounder (personal trampoline) are effective, cheap tools to use at home.

Best of all, remember that if you feel lethargic, angry, or stressed out by the kids, exercise is the best way to make you feel energized and full of vitality!

without regular exercise, your fitness declines rapidly

omega-6 fatty acids
A type of polyunsaturated fatty acid found in olives, nuts and seeds.

osteoporosis
A condition in which the density of the bones declines, making them brittle and prone to fracture.

overload
To bring about effective training, overload must be attained. This is achieved by exercising at a level that forces the muscles to work harder than they usually do. Only by achieving overload will fitness and stamina develop.

pectorals
The muscles of the chest area which are used to move the arms forwards and across the body, and to rotate the arms inwards.

pelvic floor
A hammock of muscles supporting the bladder, bowels and uterus.

pelvis in neutral
A position that supports the curves of the spine and maintains correct spinal alignment (*see p*.18).

pelvic tilt
An action that works the abdominals (*see p*.24).

principles of fitness training
Duration, frequency and intensity are the three principles involved.

protein
Protein, found in various food sources, provides the raw materials (amino acids) for growth and repair in the body. Proteins form the structure of muscles, tissues and organs. In certain circumstances, protein can be converted into glucose and used as energy.

quads/quadriceps
The four muscles at the front and sides of the thighs which are used to straighten the legs.

relaxin
A hormone that is released into the body during pregnancy to allow the pelvis to accommodate the unborn baby and the pelvic floor to stretch during delivery.

repetition
A single, completed movement of an exercise.

resistance training
The use of weights and/or body weight to tone and build muscles.

reversibility
A gradual decline in fitness that occurs when you stop exercising.

saturated fat
Oil and fat that is found mainly in dairy and meat products and chemically processed foods. This unhealthy fat can fur up the arteries and lead to heart disease.

soft knees
Keeping the knees relaxed and slightly bent rather than locked.

tendons
Non-elastic tissue bundles that attach muscles to bone.

unsaturated fat
The healthiest form of fat, found in olive oil, fish, nuts, seeds and grains. It is essential for the healthy functioning of the body.

useful addresses

Please note that, due to the fast-changing nature of the World Wide Web, some websites may be out of date by the time you read this.

The National Childbirth Trust (NCT)
Alexandra House
Oldham Terrace
Acton
London W3 6NH
Tel: 0870 444 8707
www.nctpregnancyandbabycare.com/

Association of Chartered Physiotherapists in Obstetrics and Gynaecology
11 Bayview Road
Aberdeen AB2 6BY

La Leche League
BM3424,
London WC1N 3XX
Tel: 020 7242 1278
www.laleche.org.uk

Fitness Professionals
Kalbarri House 107–113
London Road
London E13 0DA
Tel: 0870 5133434
www.fitpro.com
For current fitness developments and training.

Proactive Health Limited
Quarry Court
Bel Lane
Cassington
Oxon OX29 4DS
Tel: 01865 886300
www.proactive-health.co.uk
For all fitness equipment.

National Osteoporosis Society
Manor Farm
Skinner's Hill
Camerton
Bath
BA2 0PJ
Tel: 01761 471771
www.nos.org.uk

Getting Back Ltd
PO Box 1051
Oxford OX2 7YE
To order a video of *Getting Back* call 01865 558833
www.gettingback.co.uk

www.patrickholford.com
Resource for information on optimum nutrition.

National Library of Medicine
www.pubmed.com

www.gymguide.co.uk
Directory of health, fitness, sports and leisure clubs in the UK.

www.bodyactive-superstore.co.uk
Online store for equipment and clothing.

www.bodysolid.co.uk
For fitness equipment, including weights.

www.sweatshop.co.uk
Order running gear or get advice on running, plus useful links.

index

acknowledgments

author's acknowledgments

I would like to thank Helen Higgs, a great friend and working partner. Helen was crucial to the making of the *Getting Back* video and was the instigator of this book. Thank you to Corinne Roberts for making this book possible. Thank you to Susannah Steel who has remained calm and patient during my steep learning curve. Phew, it's done! Thank you to Nick Harris for his understanding of movement and technical wizardry, and thank you to Liz Coghill and all the team at DK for producing a book that I am proud to be a part of. Big thanks to Ruth Jenkinson, a brilliant photographer and a treat to work with, and to Kerry for her wicked humour and talent in the kitchen. Thanks to models Viven and Helena – you look fantastic. Dr. Chris A'Court has always given me help and advice, and is a great mate – thanks. Closer to home, huge thanks to Rick Boxall, who is a rock. Thank you Mary Young, Christine Webb, Belle my whiz-kid IT consultant, and to Clint for sorting everything out and making me laugh.

Deborah Mackin currently lives in Andalucía and Oxford with her three children and continues to work in fitness and dance.

publisher's acknowledgments

Dorling Kindersley would like to thank Sally Smallwood for all her work planning and directing the photo shoot and Ruth Jenkinson for the great photos. Thanks also to Caroline Buckingham for her help in setting up the project, Lyndel Costain for advising on the nutrition section and Salima Hirani for editorial assistance.

Models Deborah Mackin, Helena Bradwell, Viven Noakes and baby Alyanna, baby India (daughter of Mary Doherty Young), Lola Forsyth (baby on jacket), Carey Johnson (model on jacket), Clinton, Bella, Toby and Florence Mackin and Pat Mackin.
Illustrations Debbie Maizels
Index Dorothy Frame